A Place for Us
Gay Life at Chicago's Belmont Rocks

Owen Keehnen

Author of Man's Country: More Than a Bathhouse
&
Gay Chicago Memories: 1300 N. Wells

Rattling Good Yarns Press, LLC
33490 Date Palm Drive 3065
Cathedral City CA 92235
USA
www.rattlinggoodyarns.com

Cover Photograph: Lee Newell
Poem "Rock of Ages," courtesy of Gregg Shapiro. Copyright © 2026 Gregg Shapiro.

Library of Congress Control Number: 2026936838
ISBN: 978-1-968983-02-4

First Edition

Other Books by Owen Keehnen

Non-Fiction

Gay Chicago Memories, 1300 N. Wells St.

Man's Country, More Than a Bathhouse

LGBTQ+ Icons: A Celebration of LGBTQ+ Icons in the Arts—
Illustrations by David Lee Csicsko, Text by Owen Keehnen

Tell Me About It 3 – Editor, with St Sukie de la Croix

Tell Me About It 2 – Editor, with St Sukie de la Croix

Tell Me About It – Editor, with St Sukie de la Croix

Dugan's Bistro and the Legend of the Bearded Lady

The LGBTQ Book of Days — Revised 2019 Edition

Vernita Gray: From Woodstock to the White House—with Tracy Baim

We're Here, We're Queer

Jim Flint: The Boy From Peoria—with Tracy Baim

Leatherman: The Legend of Chuck Renslow—with Tracy Baim

Nothing Personal: Chronicles of Chicago's LGBTQ Community 1977-1997—co-editor.

Fiction

Watch Me!

Night Visitors

Love Underground

The Matinee Idol

Young Digby Swank

The Sand Bar

Doorway Unto Darkness

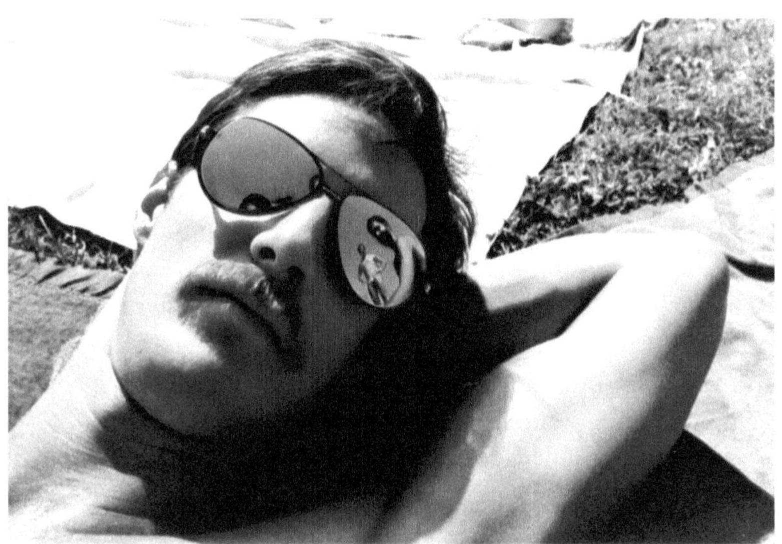

The Belmont Rocks in the 1970s was a world unto itself and a gathering place for Chicago's LGBT community for decades. Photo: William E. Kelly.

Foreword

Years before the Stonewall Inn rebellion, the Belmont Rocks was a gathering spot for Chicago LGBTQ folks to call their own. The Belmont Rocks were the limestone slabs that extended along the lakefront from the mouth of Belmont Harbor to the Lincoln Park Gun Club, just north of Diversey Harbor. The Rocks also included the lawn area east of the bike path along this stretch. Although undesirable as a beach, this inhospitable parcel of land was claimed by Chicago's gay community as their own from approximately 1960 until the Belmont Rocks were closed to the public in 2003.

Given the widespread homophobia of the era, the existence of a place like the Belmont Rocks—where gay people congregated publicly outdoors—was nothing short of revolutionary. The Belmont Rocks was a place of empowerment where gay folks asserted their right to be there, their right to exist, and their right to gather outside in the sunlight at a time when gay bars had blacked-out windows.

As a result, a *community* formed at the Rocks. Relationships and friendships developed there. It served as a gathering place—a site for cookouts, get-togethers, hook-ups, unions, memorials, dance parties, faerie time, sobriety fellowship, and more. Artwork covered many of these stones, turning the Rocks into an open-air art gallery. Although the lakefront park technically closed at 9 p.m., people came here 24 hours a day.

When I happened upon the Belmont Rocks in 1985, I thought I had found a slice of heaven with a very loose dress code: music, some pot smoke, and an almost combustible sexual energy filled the air. The area was alive with social activity. I returned the following day and the day after that. The Rocks were a place to be free—a fun, sexy, and frequently outrageous place to call our own. At the Rocks, I made friends and found my entry into the community. The freedom and acceptance there changed my life.

In the early 2000s, a decree by the Army Corps of Engineers sealed the fate of the Belmont Rocks. The area needed to be rebuilt as part of a revetment project to prevent shoreline erosion. As a result, the Rocks were demolished in 2003.

In 2017, I started working in Lakeview again after being out of the neighborhood for years. One sunny spring day, I rode my bike along the lakefront to work and arrived early. With extra time on my hands, I headed to the area that was formerly the Rocks. Veering from the bike path, I rode across the lawn and over that familiar ridge. What I saw next hit me like a punch in the gut. I was aware that the lakefront in the area had been redone, but until that moment, I hadn't absorbed the loss.

Some of the old rocks had been preserved and repurposed for seating nearby. Though a valiant attempt, a few limestone blocks were not the Belmont Rocks. The former "queerspace" felt sterilized—stripped of its magic along with all the art, energy...and the people. The sense of community that made the area so special was gone.

I took a picture of the area that day and posted it on Facebook alongside a photo of the Rocks I had taken decades earlier, and posed the question, "Are the Rocks dead?" The response to the post was overwhelming. I had no idea that my own connection to the place would resonate with so many others. When I got home, I rummaged through an old box of pictures and found a few taken at the Rocks—people lounging, partying, a Fourth of July picnic, etc.

Almost immediately, people began sending photos and sharing memories about the Rocks—recalling distant summers, lost friends, and what the place

The landscape of the Belmont Rocks in the late 1980s (top) and the area that was the Belmont Rocks after the 2003 shoreline revetment plan (below).

meant to them. There was such passion in the sharing of stories and pictures that the need to preserve the fading memory of the Belmont Rocks was evident. *A Place for Us: Gay Life at Chicago's Belmont Rocks*, was a project that found itself.

The surge of energy behind preserving the history of the Belmont Rocks was a community effort, and it was thrilling to collect some of the stories and energy of the place. One thing was clear early in the interviews—the Belmont Rocks meant many different things to people. My goal with this book is to capture as many memories as possible of that sacred space to show the varied roles it played in the lives of gay people. I collected Belmont Rocks stories for a year and a half. During this time, plans for AIDS Garden Chicago, which was to be built on the site of the Belmont Rocks, moved from the planning to the active stage. The 30-foot Keith Haring sculpture, *Self-Portrait,* was erected as part of the first phase. With the planning of the Garden, there was a renewed interest in the history of the site.

Then COVID happened, causing delays. The groundbreaking AIDS Garden Chicago eventually came in 2021, and a year to the day later, on June 2, 2022, it was officially opened with a ribbon-cutting ceremony attended by Mayor Lori E. Lightfoot, Governor J.B. Pritzker, and assorted dignitaries.

During the COVID years, I put the Belmont Rocks book on hold. Much of the issue was the cost of reproducing many of the dozens of color photos I had been sent by so many people. Temporarily daunted that the project wasn't feasible in a color format, I started a couple of other projects.

In the summer of 2024, I knew I needed to finish this book. Time was a powerful motivator. Personal histories of the Rocks were becoming an

A view of the lawn area adjacent to the Belmont Rocks on a lazy summer day, a slice of paradise.

increasingly fragile resource. In addition, as the political administration changed, the censorship of LGBTQ stories and history became a chilling possibility. Finishing the book became a priority.

As a result, I conducted dozens of additional interviews to make this retrospective of the Belmont Rocks even richer. My hope is that *A Place for Us: Gay Life at the Belmont Rocks*, will serve as a form of time travel— sparking fond memories for those who frequented the place and offering a window for those who never had the opportunity.

A percentage of the proceeds from this book will be donated to the care and upkeep of AIDS Garden Chicago.

For more information about AIDS Garden Chicago, including donation opportunities as well as a link to the AIDS stories archive, please visit the AIDS Garden Chicago website at: www.AIDSGardenChicago.org

The Stories

"What memories it all brings back," said F in 2018. As a 90-year-old gay man, F chose to remain anonymous due to his housing situation. He arrived in Chicago by way of New York and served three years in the US Army after spending the first 18 years of his life living abroad. "I was a natural-born US citizen who decided after World War II ended that the USA was where I wanted to live, and it was not always as easy as I thought it should have been.

"However, early in 1951, I met the man with whom I would spend the next 47 years living a life of absolute contentment, pleasure, love and affection, and wonder and awe on a daily basis. In the summer, that meant going to the Belmont Rocks on weekends (mostly Sundays) loaded down with coolers filled with food and drink and meeting our friends with whom we were free to be ourselves, to enjoy each other's company, and have a great time."

F continued, "We lived in Berwyn and always drove to the Rocks early in the morning so that we could secure a good parking space for the car. It was the one place and time when we could truly be ourselves, and even now, so many years later, when I look at photographs of those great and carefree days on the Rocks, the memories are almost overwhelming.

"Looking back on it now, this brings back memories and feelings of joy and fun we could only openly express when we were on the Rocks."

F added, "My sweetheart of a companion for all these many years loved going there whenever we had a chance. Being able to show his love and affection for me in this public location only added to all the good times we spent there."

The area was once the site of Nike Missile Silos. The US Army started constructing these bunkers in the area in the early 1950s during the Korean War, and deep into the Cold War. Nike missiles served as defensive weapons.

They were the first surface-to-air guided missile system developed by the US during the Cold War to protect against Russian bombers armed with nuclear weapons that could reach the interior of the country. Several Nike missile sites were installed around major metropolitan areas—including about 20 in Chicago.

In 1958, *The Chicago Tribune* reported, "The first army Nike Hercules guided missile, capable of firing a nuclear warhead against enemy bombers attacking Chicago, may be ready for action by the end of this month, it was learned yesterday.

"Headquarters of the 45th artillery brigade (air defense), at Arlington Heights, confirmed that conversion of the Nike Ajax site at Belmont Harbor to a dual-purpose Nike Ajax-Hercules battery is almost complete.

"Belmont Harbor is the first of the 21 Nike sites in the Chicago-Gary defense area to be converted to its dual purpose. Last January, Brig. Gen. Peter Schmick, brigade commander, said the newer Nike Hercules would begin protecting the area in June.

"The Hercules, according to the army announcement, has three times the range, twice the altitude, and twice the speed of the Ajax, the first Nike missile. Unlike the Ajax, it is capable of either a nuclear or high implosive warhead..." ('City's First Nike Hercules Unit Nearing Completion,' *The Chicago Tribune*, June 24, 1958).

"Atomic weapons are now protecting Chicago.

"The army unveiled at Belmont Harbor Friday the Nike-Hercules, the first anti-aircraft missile capable of firing a nuclear warhead. It will eventually replace the Nike-Ajax missile capable of firing only conventional warheads. ..."

"The Hercules has a total length of 40 feet, including a 27-foot warhead, and weighs five tons, compared to the 33-foot, one-ton Ajax. ..." ('City's Defense Bolstered by Nike-Hercules,' *The Chicago Tribune*, August 30, 1958).

"The army said today it intends to retain the Nike Hercules missile site which abuts Belmont Harbor in Chicago as a 'vital part' of the city's defense against air attack." ('Army Will Retain Nike Site at Belmont Harbor, *The Chicago Tribune*, May 3, 1961).

Noted artist Robert Middaugh (1935-2011) and his lover, Gerald Torn, sunning at the Belmont Rocks in 1962.

Larry Simpson first went to the Belmont Rocks in 1962. He had recently graduated from college, got his first "real" job, and had moved into a small, furnished apartment near Clark and Diversey. "I also was finally realizing that I was gay and accepting it. A friend told me about the Belmont Rocks. As it was a short walk from where I lived, I started spending my weekend days there to sunbathe and look.

"I usually lay on a flat rock on the second tier down where I could watch guys going back and forth between the lake and the lawn," said Simpson. "And occasionally I would spot a nude on the lower levels. Like a gopher, I'd pop up my head to see what was happening on the lawn, where there always was a bevy of activity. On July 4, 1962, I happened to look up to see, like a vision, a handsome man with a V-shaped torso and blond hair. But we said nothing, and he left."

That evening, Larry went out to get something to eat in the neighborhood. "By fortuitous coincidence or divine intervention, I passed the aforementioned male, seemingly loitering outside the Chesterfield Bar (2829-31 N. Clark). He maintains that he wasn't near the bar, but nonetheless, he was out for air along Clark Street. He started following me. After some reluctance on my part, he struck up a conversation with me. He invited me to his apartment to snack there. We'll do a fade out here.

"We started dating and I moved in with him the next spring. We now live in a high-rise even closer to the Rocks, so I continued with my sunbathing there for many years thereafter. We eventually married in 2014, when it became legal to do so in Illinois. This past 4th of July, Ed and I celebrated our 55th anniversary of meeting."

A 1960s gathering of friends at the Belmont Rocks.

Jack Fritscher only went to Belmont Rocks a couple of times in 1964 to check out the lay of the land. "I found the terrain a rather open and harsh rockscape and not conducive, as far as my inexperienced cruising eye could determine, for on-site sex— which was available 24/7 all up and down the shoreline parks and bike paths and cottages there in the early 1960s, I experimented and educated myself with cruisey sex before I ever dared meet anyone personally or go to a gay bar.

"However, back in those days when film was expensive and I lived at 60 East Chicago (nearer to other parks/beaches), I did shoot one lovely transparency of a handsome man in swim trunks standing out radiant in the open sun at the Belmont Rocks. I harvested men with cameras before I ever cruised them."

Ron Fritsch moved to Chicago on January 1, 1965. "At that time, the gay area of the Belmont Rocks was immediately to the south of the United States Army's Belmont Harbor Nike anti-aircraft missile launch site. The army maintained such sites in and around every large American city," he explained in 2017.

"More than twenty launch sites were in the Chicago area. Their purpose was to launch missiles to destroy any aircraft from the Soviet Union headed toward the city with nuclear weapons. The sites were a grim feature of the reality of the Cold War.

"Only a woven-wire fence separated the Belmont Harbor Nike missile launch site from the Belmont Rocks," explained Fritsch. "Visitors to the Rocks could easily view the soldiers at the launch site going about their business.

"I can remember being at the Rocks when the soldiers at the missile site went through a readiness drill. One such occasion was a sunny and warm weekend afternoon. A large crowd of people had gathered at the Rocks. A launcher ordinarily lay hidden in a horizontal position on the launch site with a Nike missile on top of it. In the readiness drill, the doors above the missiles and launchers opened, and the launchers with their missiles rose until they were perpendicular to the launch site," said Fritsch. "The drill captured the full attention of the visitors to the Rocks that day. When the launchers were fully erect, so to speak, the crowd sent up a loud cheer. The soldiers, who were equally amused, joined in the cheering.

"I have no personal knowledge of what took place at night at the Rocks. I heard, though, from individuals I considered to be reliable sources of such information, that the woven-wire fence was sometimes the scene of mutually enjoyable encounters between soldiers at the launch site and visitors to the Rocks.

"After the site was closed, the lakefront property it had occupied became— appropriately, I thought—part of what the next generation assumed was always the Belmont Rocks."

Looking north from the southern end of the Belmont Rocks. Photo courtesy of Alex P.

Robert Vanderschaaf first started hanging out at the Belmont Rocks in the mid-to-late 1960s..."And even though the big crowds came later, in the 1970s and 1980s, there was already action, as we say. It used to be a Nike missile base, complete with a building and servicemen. It was a bit scary when the missiles would rise up—it was just a test, but it got your attention, and of course, we would make comments regarding things 'sticking up' etc.

"This was at the very end of the 'Cold War' with Russia.

"I remember the servicemen used to sit behind the building that was there and be most entertained by watching the fairies cavorting about. I even heard stories that there was action through the chain-link fence in the dark of the night...but these were just rumors.

"Since I was a regular fixture there for many summers...I have a huge collection of memories of events and people that I knew. I truly wonder sometimes where all those people are that I knew in those days. Since I'm 73, I would assume that a great number of them are gone. What wonderful and fond memories I have of those fun-filled, far-off summer days!"

The first time David Roy Cohea went to the Belmont Rocks was in 1970. "It was prime time, middle of the afternoon on a weekend. I was in shock. The place was so festive. The Rocks were like some gay fair, something I had never seen. I had no idea such things existed. People were cooking out. There was music and dancing. There were people selling food and beer and drugs and T-shirts. Some entrepreneurs were selling things but socializing and cruising were the main things.

"By the next summer, I was a regular there. The Rocks were a huge part of my life and the lives of my friends from 1971-1976. There was such freedom there. The Belmont Rocks were like the Wild West. There was freedom from so many things that were taboo a few years before—sex, drugs, kissing...

"I would meet friends there around 11-11:30 a.m. My group was made up of night creatures—we were bartenders, waiters, drag queens, and people who worked nights and had time off during the day. When we first got there, we did very little talking. People were either still exhausted or hungover, so our group usually started with an hour nap or so, then we would get up and socialize. People would see people and go chat with other groups. We either brought lunch or bought something there. Someone was usually selling sandwiches. We would stay as late as we could, but usually everyone in our group would start to leave at 5 p.m. or 6 p.m. to get ready for their night jobs. Some days, though, we stayed until the sun went down.

"When I went, I had my special spot on the grass near the edge of the Rocks. One day in 1971, I went there, and someone was in my spot. I told him that it was my usual spot, and he told me that if I wanted to lie here, I had to share. ...We met that day and fell in love, and James and I were together for 14 years until he passed away in 1985.

"We went there together after that, but we were both very independent and had a lot of different groups, so sometimes we went together, sometimes alone, and hung out with friends or neighbors.

"The yachts would come close to shore, and guys would shout from the boat. When we were invited for a ride, my friends swam out and had a great time, but I couldn't swim, so I stayed on the Rocks.

"One afternoon, something bit me, and my knee swelled up like a balloon. One of my friends, Ray, who was a stripper in school to be a nurse, knew what needed to be done. A large crowd formed around us and cheered him on as he lanced this huge swelling on my knee.

More pre-Stonewall photos from the early 1960s at the Belmont Rocks.

"The Rocks were a good mix of people, and there were a lot of lesbians there as well. There was more safety at the Rocks than there was at the bars, but in the early 1970s, especially around 1972, there were a lot of raids on the Rocks. The cops would drive up on the grass and then run down the Rocks to try and catch people nude or having sex, or smoking pot. My friend Michael and I almost got busted there for smoking a doobie. [Once] the cops did a 'sneak attack' and I saw him at the last minute and flicked the joint as far as I could. He was saying, 'I can smell it.' He detained us, but there was no evidence.

"There was real camaraderie, too, even among the straight people who went there, who were mostly artists and bohemians and outcasts of a different kind. The camaraderie, the belonging, and the feeling of being comfortable were overwhelming. The secret would be hard to bottle."

My Time at the Belmont Rocks
By Mark Sherkow

The first time I was on the Belmont Rocks, I did not realize it was a gay area. I was 24 years old, it was a Sunday afternoon in the summer of 1970, and it turned out to be the last time I went out with a woman before I came out. We were on a daytime date; she lived nearby, and we walked to the lakefront and spread out a blanket on the grass to get some sun and talk. After a while, she looked around and then said to me, "I just realized that all the other people on the grass here are men." I glanced around—afraid to look too closely, I think—and saw that she was right.

Since that date was my last gasp at trying to be heterosexual, it didn't take long before I was coming to this area as one of the guys. For the next four years, while I lived within walking distance of the Rocks, I would visit maybe once or twice a month when the weather was warm. Even after I moved further north along the lake, I still drove down from time to time over the next few years.

I would bring a blanket, suntan lotion, and something to read. I would wear shorts and a T-shirt; sometimes I would have a bathing suit under the shorts and a towel to dry myself after taking a dip in the lake. I came when there were sure to be other guys, during the day on a Saturday or Sunday. Sometimes I came with a friend. Often, I would see people I knew, since I had started meeting other gay men at the Chicago Gay Alliance House on Elm Street, just east of Clark Street, as well as at the bars. (The Chicago Gay Alliance Community Center at 171 W. Elm was Chicago's first gay community center.)

"If it was a sunny day, there would normally be a fair number of guys there during the peak hours of the day, from 11 a.m. or 12 p.m. until 2 p.m. or 3 p.m. I came to see and talk with other people I knew, look at guys, and get some sun and relax.

"Once, singer Johnny Mathis, known to be gay, was there, sitting on a blanket with one or two other guys. A lot of us seemed to be taking looks in his direction. Finally, someone got up the courage to go talk with him. I was not close enough to hear any of the conversation. They talked for maybe 15 minutes, and then the guy went back to his own blanket.

"One time when I was feeling more self-confident than normal, I went to the Rocks early, maybe 11 a.m., and saw a friendly–looking guy sitting alone on a blanket. I approached and asked if I could set my blanket next to his. He said that was fine, and we ended up talking. It turned out he was training to be a ballet dancer; I remember he told me how hard ballet dancing was on the leg muscles. I ended up going with him to his place. I don't know if we would have had sex if it were just the two of us, but while we were there, the doorbell rang, and a very cute young man who had had sex previously with the ballet dancer dropped by, unannounced. Before long, all three of us were in the bedroom. (I think it was the only time I ever was part of a "three-way").

"To me, over the years, the Belmont Rocks were as much a part of the Chicago gay scene as the bars, the gay centers and other gay activities, the gay churches, and the gay neighborhoods.

I was shocked when I found out years later that it no longer existed as a part of our gay community."

The remaining Nike missile sites, including those near the Rocks, were contracted for demolition on July 9, 1971. Ten days later, the two contracted wrecking companies began work. The following day, *The Chicago Tribune* reported, "Massive crane begins task of digging out missile storage bays at Belmont Harbor Nike site.

"Wrecking crews from two companies are demolishing four Army Nike sites in Lincoln and Jackson Parks so the land can be returned to the Chicago Park District for recreational use. ...

"Demolition is to be finished by early next month, a Park District spokesman said. Then the 40 acres of land are to be restored to the green landscaping that was there before 1954 when the Army leased the land." ('Nike Sites Demolished,' *The Chicago Tribune*, July 20, 1971).

"The Belmont Rocks were the secret everyone knew about," said Joe Tully, who frequented the Rocks for one year, the summer of 1972. "The cutest guys at the time, the ones most admired, had a lean muscle body—a swimmer's build. The first time I went there, I was so intimidated. I weighed 140 pounds and looked like I was about 14. My first thought was, I'm out of my league with all those swimmer bodies lying in the sun and looking pretty. It was intimidating at first, but I'm pretty social, and after I started meeting people, I wasn't intimidated anymore. And it was easy to meet people at the Rocks.

"In 1972, the Rocks had bushes and trees in the lawn there. The Rocks were more cruisy then." Tully left Chicago in that year. When he returned to the city in 1976, he noticed that four years had brought changes at the Rocks—quite a few of the bushes and trees in the area had been removed, probably in an effort to curtail sexual activity.

"When I left town in 1972, the police had been cracking down at the Rocks, but it always felt like something they did when they were bored of raiding gay bars. I was never arrested up there, but I saw it happen twice that summer. People talked. They warned other people. When you went there, people would say, 'The cops are around today, be careful, mind your P's and Q's.'"

Tully continued, "When the cops rounded up some guys, they didn't usually charge them with anything. Not that I heard of anyway. They just took them to Town Hall [3600 N. Halsted]. Usually, they didn't even hold them, but there were two holding cells in the basement. They kept people there for a while. From what I remember, most people were dismissed right away. People talked at the Rocks. You got news about what happened. Information was shared."

The Belmont Rocks amid 1976 Bicentennial fever. Note the stars and stripes Speedo. Photo by John O'Brien

George Brophy started going to the Rocks in the mid-1970s. "My husband, Marty Enright, and I used to go there. We met in 1975 when I was 25 and he was 45. We used to go there on weekends—two or three times a month.

"The first time I saw them, I thought, 'This is so cool!' Actually, my first thought when we arrived at the Rocks was, 'Where are we going to park?' The Rocks was a popular spot, a place to see and to be seen. We made a big impression. We turned heads with the 20-year age difference—I was young and cute, and Marty was handsome and so butch.

"At the Rocks, there was always music; there were people playing volleyball, people spread out on blankets and towels. There was the lakefront and the skyline. It was beautiful. Further down on the rocks themselves, things were cruisier. Sometimes the guys down there would be naked."

Brophy also recalled the boats that would anchor off the Rocks. "I never swam out to a boat, but I was on boats that people swam out to. They would come on board, have a beer with us, socialize, and then go back to the Rocks or sometimes stay on board.

"After my husband, Marty, and I opened Buddies [3301 N. Clark St.], we would have bar picnics down there. Buddies sponsored a couple of men's softball teams and a couple of women's softball teams. We had two of our teams advance to the championships. The teams sometimes had practice at the Rocks, and some games were there too, so a few of us would often bring a cooler down there to watch the Buddies team and show support."

Brophy was unsure of the last time he went to the Rocks before the limestone slabs were demolished. "Nothing really happened that I recall, but somewhere along the line, going to the Rocks just faded, the Rocks became less popular, and everyone started moving north to Hollywood Beach."

In 1975, William (Bill) E. Kelly (Not to be confused with gay activist Bill Kelley) was 28 and had just been honorably discharged from a four-and-a-half-year tour in the Air Force. "...The unpopular Vietnam War was winding down. My society and family-approved heterosexual marriage was also coming to a close. With Cocker Spaniel, clothes, and personal papers packed into a 1972 Ford Pinto, my 1100-mile journey of introspection and self-discovery began. Thoughts of how my life would continue or if it should, ricocheted wildly through my mind. It was a terrifying time when I began to realize I had been living the life others expected while sacrificing my true self. But who was my true self? What would living it mean?

"Arriving home in suburban Chicago, I shared only that my wife and I were divorcing. Little more was said. I took a job in the local paper mill, where I had worked summers, and spent the next year coming to understand who I was and what kind of life I wanted to live. A year and a half later, in 1977, I moved into Chicago, made friends, and set out to find the lasting relationship I wanted."

The first time William Kelly went to the Belmont Rocks, he thought, "Wow, a place where we can be ourselves in the daytime. People were free there, and on weekends, there were probably 300-400 people. It felt so freeing

Friends clowning in the surf at the Belmont Rocks in the 1970s (top) and clowning on the lawn (bottom). Courtesy of William E. Kelly, a community activist who relocated to California in the late 1970s.

to be there. I went to the Rocks every sunny weekend that I could when I wasn't travelling. I was still looking for a husband, and soon after, I met my partner, Bob. I didn't meet him at the Rocks; I tell people we met in the Bushes. It's a good line, but I'm talking about the bar. [The Bushes, 3320 N. Halsted St.] We were both there for an event with the Lincoln Park Lagooners, and we both ended up doing quite a bit with the group."

After meeting at the Bushes, Bob and Bill became companions, confidants, partners, and lovers. "So, then Bob and I went to the Rocks together, and we had friends who went there. Sometimes we would bring food and have a party with six to ten other people. We didn't have a specific spot to meet, but we all just knew where to look for one another. Usually, we set up closer to the Rocks than the bike path, about 20 yards from the top row of stones.

"We would eat, and sometimes we would play cards, but mostly it was about conversation and being together. The Rocks were a place to laugh and talk with our friends about our lives and our problems as well. Any topic was open for discussion. ...We shared our dreams, stories, and troubles. We laughed, cried, comforted each other, drew strength from, and relished the true community we created. Little did we know that hundreds of those we knew and planned to grow old with would perish in their prime from HIV/AIDS. They were never to experience non-discrimination laws, marriage equality, open military service and civil equality and freedoms, or societal acceptance at any level."

The Belmont Rocks were a place to find out what was going on in the community and a popular place for friends to gather and unwind. The Belmont Rocks in 1973. Photo courtesy of Phil.

William Lutz was in his mid-20s when he moved to Chicago in 1974. He first visited the gay beach in the summer of 1975. "There were two gay beaches. One was on the concrete north of the Oak Street beach from Division northward. This area had long been a gathering spot, drawing from the large gay population in Old Town to the west, and that beach area was known as 'The Slabs.' The other beach was farther north, the area officially known as the Belmont Rocks, or just 'The Rocks' to the gay community. Gays had recently moved in large numbers into the area immediately to the west of what was then called New Town.

"The Rocks had ideal geography and access, located between the barriers of the harbor and its parking lot to the north, and the gun club that shot skeet out into the lake to the south. Strangely, the site had once been home to a Nike missile base, intended to protect Chicago from a Soviet Union attack from 1955 to 1965. During those years, it was isolated, and the Rocks were a magnet for gay cruising. The area reverted to parkland when the base was torn down."

Lutz described the Rocks as an island unto itself. "At that point, the Drive swings to the west, and the bike/pedestrian path was far enough away from view that the gay beach goers felt more 'unseen' and could be more natural among each other. It sounds quaint today, but this was an important aspect. The pedestrian access under the Drive at Barry provided a shortcut vs. having to use Diversey or Belmont, especially if on foot.

"During those years, it was isolated and continued as a magnet for gay cruising and sunbathing. As word spread, by 1976, more and more of the gay community from other than New Town made the trek (usually by bicycle) from elsewhere on the North Side. Of course, using the word 'beach' was a misnomer, because there was no sand, just grass and the hard pavement of the rocks...

"Yes, there were those straight walkers who would decide to turn towards the water as they passed the gun club. It was amusing to watch their reaction, first on their faces, then on whether they turned back to the asphalt path or not. The cops stayed away in the early days, and the vendors with a cooler full of beer sold them by the can and were mostly left alone. Later on, the police on four-wheelers would drive up to bust any nude sunbathing. Generally, those on the top rocks would shout the alert to get your clothes on.

"The Rocks quickly became a place that changed from a cruisy place for individual sunbathers to 'party central', where large groups would gather together. Several hundred would populate each sunny weekend day. There was a natural divide between the large grassy area and the stair-step rocks that descended into the lake. The former became more social, the latter more individual and cruisy. They were not mutually exclusive, as everyone migrated depending on mood, and the Rocks provided access to the water.

"The limestone rocks were built to curb erosion, primarily in the 1930s. By the 1970s, the waves had caused many to tilt and some to fall into the lake. This created large individual rocks, ideal for sunbathing down near the water for one or two people. Boats would pull up and anchor. Guys would swim ashore, and others would swim out to meet new friends.

"It was the age of the boom box, and that added greatly to the atmosphere of the place. Gays were clever in that they figured out that instead of competing boom box music, if everyone tuned into the same radio station, the entire area was filled with the same music. The greater the number of people, the greater the number of 'extended speakers' there were. The result was a stereophonic 'room.' As you walked into the space, the cooler lake breeze, the music, the laughter, and the tanned bodies lying about, it was like entering the train platform to Hogwarts.

"WLS FM 94.7 had changed from a hard rock format to disco, and the call letters became WDAI. The same music that everyone had danced to the night before in the bars was belting from the speakers, extending the atmosphere into a day party that carried on from the night before. The station played many tracks between commercials, and even played mixes created by gay DJs of the period, although these were mostly played at night.

"The individual blankets merged to become large islands like enormous quilts, with 10-20 people soaking up the sun and socializing together," continued Lutz. "It was so easy to meet new people as friends of friends were introduced. Lunches brought in knapsacks became more elaborate brunches on Sundays and were spread out for all to share as the summer wore on. People compared notes on which bars were fun and had a great DJ the previous night. Upcoming events and apartment parties were planned. One could blanket hop throughout the afternoon, and the friend-of-a-friend introductions multiplied.

"Promptly at 3 p.m., at least half the population got up and left. The sun's rays were not going to gain that extra color, and they needed a shower, a nap, and dinner before going out. During the week, the area became more laid back. There were more single sunbathers and groups of two or four friends. The crowd was 99% male, and it did have a (small) Black and Latino contingent that grew larger in the 1980s.

"The volleyball players were another attraction. Occasionally, there would be a net set up at the Rocks, but those who were serious about the game gathered across the Drive, where a group played on the east side of the North Pond/Lagoon in Lincoln Park. It was often a stop on the way home from the Rocks. This group became the Lincoln Park Lagooners...

"As the years went by, several artists began to paint on the limestone. Their creations were quite varied and colorful, and for the most part, quite good. Most were geometrical, and some even continued from the top surface down the vertical sides of the rocks. Some were small and some quite large. I don't recall anyone, including the city, objecting to these early murals. When the Army Corps of Engineers announced the construction project to replace the rocks with a concrete revetment, they promised to preserve this art. At best, only a few were saved, and most of the truly inventive ones were lost.

"Alas, like *Brigadoon*, my peak summers there were 1977-1978. Technology marched on, and the Sony Walkman killed the boom box, and the beach crowd fragmented. The larger convergence of blankets shrank back to singles and small groups. WDAI gave up its disco format in 1980. The Rocks remained a gay magnet during the summer...but not to the same extent. I can't pinpoint the year, but during the 1980s, the gay community itself shifted farther north, primarily in search of lower rents. Andersonville became popular, and the Kathy Osterman Beach became more convenient for the far North Siders."

❖ ❖ ❖

Artwork on display at the Rocks in 1991. Photo by Bill M.

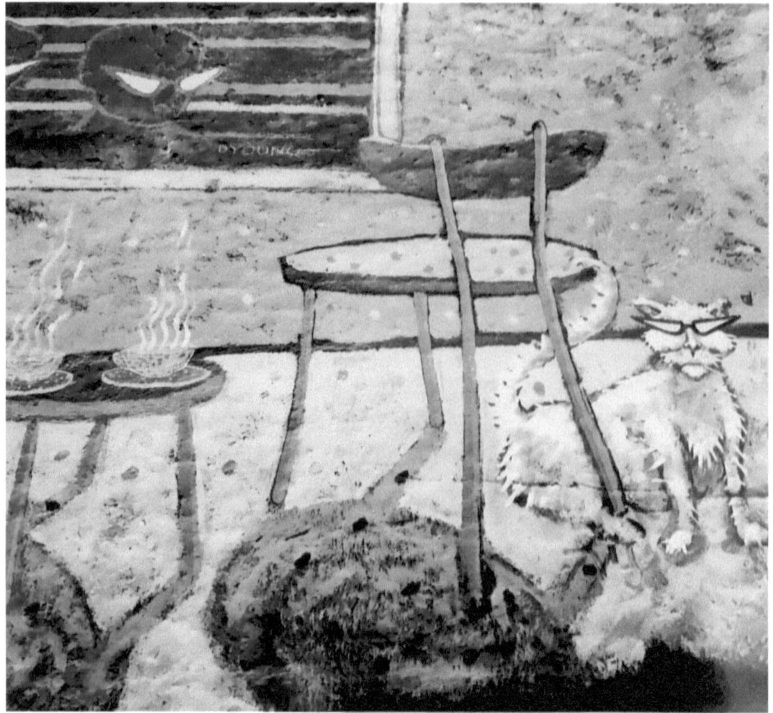

Another example of the plentiful artwork on display at the Rocks in 1991. Photo by Bill M.

In his 1994 novel, *The Beautiful Room is Empty*, award-winning author and former Chicagoan Edmund White (1940-2025) captured some of the magic of the Belmont Rocks.

"Lou was fired from his advertising job, but he told me that happened every six months anyway in the biz. 'Every time they lose a big account, they can the whole team.' I want to write a book called Love You, Love Your Work, Gonna Hafta Let You Go. Now that neither of us was working, we were free to go to the Oak Street beach every day or sometimes a mile or two farther north to some slabs of broken concrete, the Belmont Rocks, where the gay boys had staked a claim and which Lou called 'Homo-lulu.' Now I knew the whole adolescent world I'd missed out on, the world of idle summer days, of tinny portable radios and coconut oil, of towel hopping and shared Cokes, of desultory exclamations ('Ow! That bug really bit me') followed by wave-lulled silence and the indignant nursing of the glossy shoulder or silky thigh." (White, The Beautiful Room is Empty, Vintage Random House, 1994).

"I am a lesbian who spent years with my gay brothers/friends sunning on the Belmont Rocks in the 1970s," shared Lorraine. "We usually went both Saturday and Sunday, and although there were mostly men on the Rocks, we 'girls' knew we were always welcome. The weekend crowd was predictable, and we all had our 'spots.' If someone was late, we often left their spot open for them until it became clear they weren't going to come that day.

"My partner and I would go to McDonald's and get coffee and breakfast and start our weekend days in the quiet of the morning on the lake. Gradually, the Rocks would fill up with new and familiar faces. Sometimes we would get together for dinner with friends we had hung out with on the Rocks that day.

"I am still friends with two guys who were our neighbors in the early 1970s and who have now been together 40 years...although I moved to California in 1984. I also lost some of the friends we made on the Rocks to AIDS. Now that I am older, I am not allowed to forget my time of being irresponsible while sunning on the Rocks because I now sport dark 'sunspots' on my face: not attractive to be sure, but worth the memories.

"...It was not possible for a passerby to mistake the population of that portion of the lake. When women joined the men, it was usually as a couple. One of the things we had great fun with was watching heterosexual couples come upon the gathering unexpectedly and gradually realize what they had wandered into. Almost invariably, they would 'drop hands' as they walked through, and we'd all get a good laugh.

"I never did like going to bars, so there was something especially appealing about being out and open in the daylight. I never remember a problem between people," added Lorraine. "Whether or not we knew each other, we knew why we were there, and so knew we had a bond with everyone else who was there. It felt like a safe spot even before it became fashionable to be gay."

In 1974, Jim Flagler moved from the suburbs and into a place at Pine Grove and Addison in Lakeview. "At the time, I was going to the Church of the Ascension, and it was filled with gay people. So, after services, sometimes we would go out for breakfast and then for a recreational smoke at the Rocks. We would hang out there. I sunburned easily, so I tended to stay over by the south side of the Rocks, where the trees were, by the gun club. Then, when we went back to church for Evensong, we would be high as kites."

Flagler recalled, "Another time I was with a guy, and we were there in our Speedos and lying out, and a man came along and said he was a photographer and asked to take our picture. Four months later, I am riding the elevator of my building, going to work, and this guy on the elevator asked if I was going in to work that day. I said yes and thought it was an odd thing to ask. At the time, I worked at a conservative bank downtown. Then I ran into someone else who asked me the same thing but refused to give me details. Finally, someone at work showed me the latest copy of *The Reader*, and it was a cover story on Chicago's Gay Beach with me on the cover in a Speedo. I was pretty much out in my personal life by then, but this outed me professionally as well. It turned out fine in the end."

More 1970s atmosphere at the Belmont Rocks. Photo courtesy of the late Ron Ehemann (1950-2024).

Lori Cannon began to frequent the Belmont Rocks in the summer of 1977. "I would go there on outings organized by my hairstylist, so I debuted a collection of different and magnificent hairstyles at the Belmont Rocks. The Rocks was a place to lie on blankets and listen to music. There was no body shaming. It seemed like everyone fit in there. The Rocks was about community and enjoying liberation. It was about relationships, sunshine, water, friendships, and debauchery—all the things I enjoy. The Rocks were also a place to admire beauty, and at the Rocks, there was so much beauty on display. Difficult to imagine that only five or six years later, life would change for everyone, but in the late 1970s, the party at the Belmont Rocks was going strong."

Tom Chiola moved to Chicago on July 1, 1978. During his first few weeks in the city, he went for a bike ride along the lakefront. "I came upon this group of guys playing softball, and as I watched, I thought, 'This is a group I may have a few things in common with.' That summer, I started making the effort to get there for those pickup softball games. The skill level was good to horrible, but

Tom Chiola at the Belmont Rocks. Chiola became the first openly gay candidate elected to public office in the state after winning a Cook County Circuit Court judicial position in 1994.

people helped each other. If you weren't sure of the way to hold the bat, someone would help. People were encouraging, and if you got too hot, you could just go jump in the lake. The games were about camaraderie. No one cared too much about the score. Those pick-up games were how the gay softball leagues developed. After the game, we went back to people's places for barbecues. Several of those barbecues were at Bob Gammie's place."

Chiola continued. "The Rocks was our beach, so most weekends I would pedal there, turn my bicycle upside down, and put my towel down among the many others. I would be there in the latest Speedo fashion. Sometimes I would meet people, and we would leave the Rocks and go for a drink or to get something to eat somewhere. The Rocks were a place where you could put flotation devices, rafts, and inner tubes in the water, and there were no lifeguards on duty there to harass you about it. On summer days, boats would come up close, and the guys would hop in and swim out. The ice cream guy would come by, and I loved to get the pina colada and mango-flavored popsicles he sold. Those were so good."

❖ ❖ ❖

Backgammon at the Belmont Rocks in the 1980s. Photo courtesy of Frank Nichter.

Indianapolis native Frank Nichter first went to the Belmont Rocks in 1975, when he was spending the summer in Chicago. "Indy had bars, but they didn't have any place like this. I was working a 9-5 job and living at Bob Gammie's at 5333 N. Lakewood. He was the guy behind the Lincoln Park Lagooners. He had a big house and rented out rooms to gay guys coming to Chicago. He worked at the unemployment office in Evanston so he could get you a job as well. Bob was Mr. Chicago, and he used to always say, 'Every night is Saturday night in Chicago.'"

Nichter continued, "We went to the Belmont Rocks every Saturday and Sunday. We went there with our blankets and coolers. Oftentimes, we didn't get there until 1 or 2. By then, the Rocks would be completely full, so we went to the grass. Bob was fine with that. He preferred the grass. Bob brought a backgammon board. He would sit, and people would come by and talk to him and maybe play some backgammon. We would stay until 4 or 5 p.m. and go home before going out or before I had to go into work."

The following summer, Nichter moved to Chicago. A large part of his decision to relocate were the high points of his previous summer—the Lincoln Park Lagooners, Bob Gammie, and the Belmont Rocks. "The Lagooners introduced me to people, and I got to know a lot of people very fast. The gay population in Chicago seemed huge. Most of the guys in the Lagooners were in their 30s, and I was 19, so I was popular. I also played softball with them, so I got to know them all. Tuesdays at 6 p.m., we would all meet to play softball at the Belmont Rocks. Afterwards, we would go to someone's house for a barbecue, and then I would meet more people.

"The Rocks were so crowded in the 1970s. Everybody seemed to go there. For me, it was the place to be from 1975-1982. Going there was not about sex for me. Going to the Belmont Rocks was always very social. That was where my friends would always be."

"The artwork at the Rocks was amazing," added Nichter. "Such a shame it's gone. There were many peace and heart signs. People would put their names and or their boyfriend's initials. There was that kind of thing, but there were some who did amazing artwork. I used to love walking the Rocks and looking at it all. The great thing was that the art on the Rocks was always evolving— every time you walked it, there were different things to see."

Nichter continued, "Sometimes I went with people from work. I was a waiter. I remember the hot-looking guys who would go there and how they would swim out to yachts or boats that cruised near the Rocks, and then they would spend the day on a boat.

"It was pure fun and joy to smoke a joint or two and get a buzz going. And to do it without hiding, not just getting high, but being gay and being there. It just felt so open, and that was really cool."

David Plomin would drive or ride his bike to the Belmont Rocks. "The first time I went there was probably 1975-1976. I would pick up guys sometimes and go back to their place—I often came home cleaner than when I left."

When Plomin moved from home in 1977, he was eager to go to the Rocks more often. "There were so many hot guys in Speedos sunning themselves. I liked going there for boy watching. Mostly, I went alone. There were lots of groups, different cliques of people off doing their own thing. I went mostly during the week. Weekends were too crowded. I also remember all the

Frank and friends enjoying some extracurricular fun at the Rocks. Photo by Frank Nichter.

closeted guys who went there and how they would pretend that they had just happened upon the place."

Catching some rays at the Rocks in the 1980s. Photo by Lee Newell.

In 2018, Michael Bauer shared his personal experience of the Belmont Rocks. The following year, Bauer died of cancer at age 66.

"I remember as a young man in the 1970s driving my car north on Lake Shore Drive, especially on a weekday, and noticing a number of men, usually by themselves, lying on beach towels and wearing Speedos or other similar swimwear in an area east of the Drive and just north of Diversey. I never stopped because, in 1974 at the age of 21, I married a young woman, despite having same-sex relationships and even a boyfriend in college.

"Finally, I remember in 1976 parking my car far away and walking on what is now known as the Lakefront Path from Diversey to Belmont to get a better look at the men lying on the grass and on the cement. It was all so erotic and also very frightening—I was afraid to get a closer look for fear that I would run into someone who recognized me.

"Fast forward to 1979. I was now divorced and coming out fast. Carol's Speakeasy [1355 N. Wells St.] was my regular haunt on Friday and Saturday evenings. And I became a regular at the Rocks.

"Weekdays at the Rocks were very different than weekends. Weekends were usually very social. Usually, groups of men would be sitting around together, often with picnics of drinks and food. In contrast, weekdays usually saw individual men lying by themselves—men cruising for action. Often, the action would happen right there. I remember countless times seeing someone or someone seeing me, and suddenly it became erotic...

"But it was also an opportunity to make friends. The first gay friend I made after I came out was Steve T., who I met at the Rocks. We cruised each other, and he came up to me and we started chatting. Eventually, I invited him back to my apartment, where we just sat and talked for hours. We became fast friends, and he welcomed me into his circle of friends, who became the first gay circle of friends I had in Chicago.

"One of my funniest stories involved taking home a hairy, dark hunk who I met at the Rocks. After we had sex, he looked at me and said that he had been at this apartment previously. I looked closely at him and realized that we had tricked months earlier under the same circumstances!

"Weekends at The Rocks were so social, lots of time with friends and meeting friends of friends, and making new friends. But then AIDS hit Chicago around 1984 and 1985, and right away, one could tell who was infected because of the ever-present evidence of Kaposi's sarcoma. And then friends for years started to no longer show up because they were so sick, and eventually because they had passed away.

"At that point, for me, I stopped going to the Rocks. It was more haunted by ghosts than anything else and was no longer fun. But there are men, beautiful men like David S. and Kraig D., particularly come to mind, who I am still able to remember being at the Rocks before they died—memories of them with their beautiful smiles and celebrating the experience of being the first 'out' generation of men in Chicago."

In 1976, Danny Kopelson left for college and came out on the same day. Kopelson was attending the University of Illinois at Champagne, but he was an Evanston native. "I would go to the bars and the baths when I came home from school. You could drink at 19 in those days. During that time, I had gone to the Rocks, but my biggest connection to the place came after I moved to Lakeview. I lived first on Roscoe and Lake Shore Drive, then 555 Cornelia, and then 3150 Lake Shore Drive. The Rocks weren't necessarily a part of that decision but having the Rocks right there was more like a wonderful benefit to all those places."

Kopelson shared that his favorite memories from the Belmont Rocks start in 1983 and relate to his membership in the Chicago Gay Men's Chorus. "A bunch of us from the Chorus went there every weekend. We would have potlucks, and everyone would bring different kinds of food. That was the source of a running joke in the chorus. We were having one of those potlucks at the Belmont Rocks, and I was in charge of bringing dessert—they probably expected cupcakes or bakery cookies or something, but I brought a package of sugar wafers. I probably just went and bought something cheap, and that became a running joke. Whenever we had potlucks after that, someone would always bring a package of sugar wafers, or if I brought food, I would bring that, plus a package of sugar wafers.

"The Rocks were perfect for me because I loved to be in the sun, and you saw everyone there. Even being there with other Chorus members gave us a chance to talk since a lot of times at rehearsal there wasn't time to catch up."

Kopelson added, "There was just a much broader community at the Rocks in general. There were groups and guys alone cruising and hovering. For me, going there was completely social—not only being social with the Chorus, but by then I was also involved and volunteering with different AIDS groups, so I knew more people that way.

"The Belmont Rocks was the place to be, especially during the day on the weekends. It really was a joyous place for community, even during the worst years of AIDS. And then people moved north, and it was over."

"Belmont Rocks sunbathers will have new companions next summer. A statuary group depicting an Ottawa Indian family will have been moved to the popular Lakefront area from its former location at Lincoln Park Zoo. The 90-year-old statue, entitled 'Alarm,' shows the family and its dog alerted to impending danger." (Eye on the News by William B. Kelley, *The Chicago Gay Crusader*, November-December 1974).

"If you've wondered why the gay Belmont Rocks sunbathing area seems so shabby after the Nike missile base was removed, it could be because the park district spent $37,466 less on restoring the land than the $201,265 provided by the Army for that purpose. Among the shortcuts taken by the park district were the omission of a sprinkler system and substituting cheap, quick-growing grass for costlier resodding. Then the district spent the extra money elsewhere. (Other former Nike sites have similarly been shortchanged in restoration by the park district)." (Eye on the News by William B. Kelley, *The Chicago Gay Crusader*, November 1975).

The statue 'Alarm,' depicting a Native American family, stood at the southern edge of the Belmont Rocks.

In the late 1970s, Lee Newell was working the phone lines at Gay Horizons on Clark St. near Diversey. "On the phones, we were asked questions about everything, so we had to know things, that's how I knew about the Rocks. It was easy to get there from work. I would leave Horizons, walk down Diversey to the lake, and then north to the Rocks.

"When I first went, the Rocks area was in pretty rough shape. It was muddy and patchy with crabgrass. Neglected by the city. The gays went there for the same reason that early gay bars were in bad neighborhoods. As beaches went, it was bad—but we could do almost anything there. Lots of pot. The only

Summer days at the Belmont Rocks, Photo courtesy of Lee Newell

thing in those days that I remember the police cracking down on was nude swimming."

Newell went to the Belmont Rocks at least once a week during the summer if he was in town. "I went from the 1970s into the 1980s. Over time, the condition of the park improved. The area got trash barrels. There weren't any of those at first. They filled in the gaps behind the Rocks where the soil had eroded...

"I went there a few times for planned get-togethers with friends, but usually I just turned up and then looked for friends. I always found people I knew to hang out with because in those days, everyone hung out there.

"It wasn't a good place to swim," added Newell. "Most people just got in the water to cool off or went on the lower rocks and let the waves wash over them. It made sense when everything moved north, and people started going to Hollywood Beach—an actual beach with sand where you could swim. I was also a little sad when that happened because we were also losing an old tradition."

Karlis Streips grew up in Morton Grove and discovered the Belmont Rocks when he was a teenager. "I knew I was gay since I was probably nine and learned about the Belmont Rocks from swiping copies of *Gay Chicago.*

"The first time I went there, I was probably 16, so it would have been 1976. I was very shy, and so I would usually just go to the Rocks alone and bring a book."

Streips continued to go to the Belmont Rocks until about 1983. "I enjoy summer, and it was a nice place to hang out—the Rocks was a gay spot, and it was predominantly gay men, so there was plenty of eye candy."

Jim Be first went to the Belmont Rocks in 1976. "I'm sure it was with some people from the Bistro. At the time, I was sneaking in underage, and someone from there took me to the Rocks after the bar closed. I am from the South Side, and I had no idea where I was being taken. I thought it was a nude beach.

"We went there and watched the sunrise, and as it got later, more and more people began to congregate. After that, I went there every few weeks for the next decade or so, until about 1986. Sometimes I went there with friends on the weekend. Or we would go there after the bars closed to watch the sunrise, get some food, and come back. At the Rocks, some folks would take everything off, and it wasn't a big deal. I also liked the artwork there, hearts and messages in chalk, some in paint. I don't remember a lot of the art, but I remember there was a lot of it. Those were fun years."

Enjoying the sun. Photo courtesy of Marty Hyams.

Wayne and Vicky relaxing at the Belmont Rocks. Photo courtesy of Wayne Kauffmann.

❖ ❖ ❖

The first time Dave Samber went to the Belmont Rocks was in the summer of 1977. "Before then, I had a professional career, and that summer I found myself with no job. Being out of work, I went to the Belmont Rocks all the time."

Samber lived nearer downtown but would bike to the Rocks. "It was a great vista, rolling along the lakefront and then going off the path and riding over to the top of the Rocks. The water was cold, but it was a refreshing swim. I had the same Speedo I wore there for years. I was 27 at the time and in shape. It was great to go to the Rocks and not be bothered, but it was okay to get interrupted.

"I always met really good people there, interesting people from all walks of life," added Samber. "There were a lot of people that I would see every day. We all went there. Some people brought coolers, picnic baskets, candles, umbrellas—they went all out. The area smelled like coconut oil. There was a good vibe to the place, but it was by no means wholesome. It was a great place to cruise, and then you could also hide in the rocks...

"About two months later, I was offered a job. Now I had money in my pocket, but I still went back to the Rocks. It was the chance to find some companionship. Not a husband, just someone to spend time with. I would meet friends there," recalled Samber. "We would show up between 11 a.m. and 2 p.m. and spend a few hours at the Rocks. Then, when we left there, it was time for happy hour. Usually, we went to the Broadway Limited [3132 N. Broadway] and danced after being in the sun."

In the 1970s, Terence Alan Smith, aka Joan Jett Blakk, came to Chicago with a clubbing buddy from their hometown of Detroit after hearing about the gay bar Alfie's [900 N. Rush St.]. The two friends decided to make it a weekend.

"We booked into a Holiday Inn in Lincoln Park. We had a rock n roll sighting at the hotel as we were checking in, too. I happened to notice a well-dressed hippy next to me, nice, long blonde hair, totally working that rich girl bohemian look. Upon a closer study, she was very familiar in that way that famous people sometimes are, and then it hit me. I was standing next to Mary Travers, of Peter, Paul, and Mary fame. I spoke right up, 'Hello, Ms. Travers. You're looking well.' She gave a polite nod, thanked me, and floated away, all silk fabric scarves and suede boots. That made me feel we had checked into the right hotel.

"We had a fabulous time at the bar, dancing and cruising and doing a bit of coke here and there. Neither of us picked up anybody, so we went back to the hotel around 5 a.m. We had heard about this sort of beach for gay people called the Belmont Rocks, which was not too terribly far away, and that the place was always hopping. Donning our daytime attire, we soon found ourselves gliding up Lake Shore Drive toward Belmont Ave."

When Blakk and their friend, Jerry, arrived at the Belmont Rocks, the parking lot was already starting to fill despite the early hour. "We followed the crowd and soon found ourselves at the oddest-looking beach I'd ever seen. They really were rocks—steps of them leading to the water. It looked like ancient Rome or something. It stretched from Belmont Ave. on the north to Diversey Ave. to the south. Because the long slabs of concrete cascaded down to the water, the rocks were mostly obscured from the view of anyone walking by or riding past on the bike path.

"The lake was sparkling in the morning light, the roar of traffic on Lake Shore Drive was a distant hum, and there were naked boys everywhere! Well, maybe not totally naked, though some were. Mostly, it was wearing the most flattering swimwear to accentuate one's bulge. Part of the ritual was the 'ho stroll,' at least that's what my friends and I called it. The 'ho stroll' consisted of walking back and forth along the beachfront, usually on the top tier of the rocks to see and be seen. ..."

Blakk recalled, "It was already getting really hot that day, and the place was filling up with fuckable hotness. Mind you, this entire thing was hidden in plain sight near the gun club, so there was occasional shooting going on. There was a harbor there, too, so families on their way to a lovely afternoon on the new sailboat passed daytime disco queens on their way to a huge tea dance. Very interesting. Remember, this was only 1977—folks were just not ready for it. This particular Sunday morning, I'm sure many of these people had just come from some church service in Elmhurst and now were vying for parking spaces with black dykes who looked, bless them, as if they would stomp you into the ground if you so much as looked at them wrong. Actually, they were very sweet.

"As I said before," continued Blakk, "It was already starting to get rather hot, and you know gay boys, we will figure out how to look comfortable and sexy at the same time. This particular day, we were featuring the very shortest hot pants available and a plain white tank top. Yes, it was the seventies, so if shoes were worn at all, they were either plastic sandals called jellies or platform wedgies. Man candy was everywhere!

"From that day forward, the Belmont Rocks became an enchanted faerie land, neatly tucked up under the hem of Chicago's lakefront. I went there often. I went in the heat of the day, and I was there many times to see a thunderstorm roll in from the west, suddenly drenching all. I went there at night, when a full moon illuminated the still lake waters, and made the Rocks themselves seem as if they were in spotlights."

This page and next, three photos are of an arrest at the Belmont Rocks, supposedly the perpetrator was selling sandwiches without a license. Photos by Jerry Pritikin.

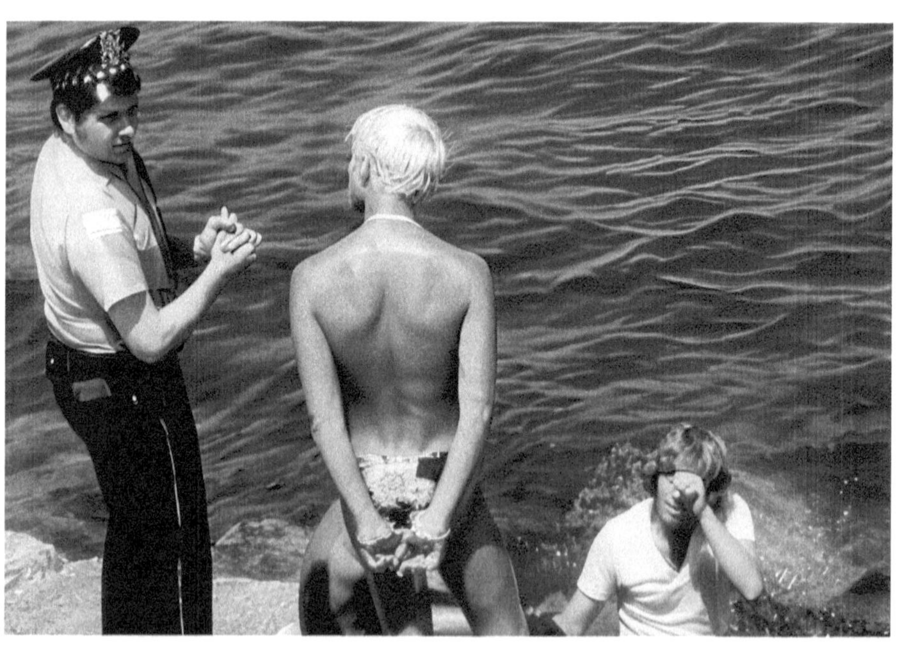

At the Belmont Rocks, the police sometimes liked to make themselves known. The usual charges for arrest were indecent exposure, open alcohol, recreational drug use, curfew, and trespassing. Sometimes there were other reasons.

In 1975, noted photographer Jerry Pritikin snapped these three photos of an arrest at the Belmont Rocks. According to Pritikin, the young man being taken away in his Speedo was busted for selling sandwiches without a license.

The August 15, 1975, issue of *Gay Life* newspaper reported the following. "Six members of the community, three of whom are employees of the Gold Coast, were arrested on Tuesday, July 29, while enjoying the sun and warm weather at the Belmont Rocks...

"What began as a harmless dialogue with a Chicago police officer in the process of writing a citation for a bike illegally parked in the area turned into a fiasco when the officer apparently panicked and called for help on the police radio.

"The guys...saw the officer writing the ticket and went to ask him about the problem, offering to move the bike. Observers at the scene had noted that the officer had previously been testy toward a hot dog vendor in the same area.

"Within two minutes of the officer's call for help, the area was swarming with eight police cars and two three-wheeler bikes. Some of the cars were filled with officers who immediately began arresting the six, charging them with 'disorderly conduct' and similar offenses.

"Dressed only in bathing suits, the six were escorted by about eighteen officers to Town Hall district station, 3600 N. Halsted St., where bond was set at $25,000 following 'booking.'

"Gay News and Events received a call at about 3 p.m. from the lover of one of the parties arrested, asking for help in raising bail money for the six. After a call to Town Hall to determine exact offenses and bond required, *Gay News* made a call to Chuck Renslow, the operator of the Gold Coast, for assistance. Renslow, located at the nearby Grubsteak Restaurant, had already been advised of the situation and was making arrangements for the release of all six.

"John Chester, a member of the Alliance to End Repression committee monitoring police behavior, contacted some of those arrested for details to present at Police Board meetings. Some of the group said they preferred to drop the matter rather than have a hassle over the 'minor incident.'" (*Gay Life.* 'Six arrested at Belmont Rocks,' August 15, 1975).

❖ ❖ ❖

Community happened at the Rocks. Photo courtesy of Marty Hyams.

The management of the gay bathhouse, Man's Country, chose the Belmont Rocks as the site for a community fundraiser—a very gay version of High School Homecoming. That weekend, the Man's Country Trojans paired off against a team from the Tavern Guild in a football game at the Belmont Rocks.

On the evening of the game, there was a big homecoming dance at the bathhouse. At the culmination of the evening, Mr. Football Hero was crowned. The competition was neither a beauty contest nor an award for athletic prowess. The title was given on the basis of fundraising. Mr. Football Hero was the guy who collected the most money for the Tavern Guild's Frank M. Rodde Memorial Building Fund. In addition to the title, Mr. Football Hero received a color television.

"Saturday, October 15, was the Mr. Football Contest at Man's Country, with all monies collected going to the Tavern Guild's Frank M. Rodde III Memorial Building Fund [The Rodde Center was a community center and a precursor to the Center on Halsted]. The Tavern Guild members played an exciting, if not murderous, football game with the guys from Man's Country at the Rocks earlier in the afternoon. So, if you wondered why some of the bartenders in town looked tired and sore, now you know.

"As a result, $400 was collected for the Rodde Fund." (Heidi Snoop, "Off-Broadway Tid-Bits," *Gay Chicago News*, October 21, 1977).

The following spring, the popular bathhouse repeated the format for a softball-based fundraiser. The big game was once again held at the Belmont Rocks. This time, the Man's Country Trojans were pitted against the Lincoln Park Lagooners. The beneficiary of the event was the Pride Week Committee. As with football homecoming, the softball game was followed by a celebratory dance at Man's Country. That evening, a Mr. Baseball Hero was named. To earn the title this time, contestants had two hours to raise the money...by whatever means necessary. Whoever raised the most money for the Pride Week Committee received $100, a year's pass to Man's Country, and the title of Mr. Baseball Hero.

Party in progress at the Belmont Rocks. Photo courtesy of Ron Ehemann.

Jim Huberty went to the Belmont Rocks for the first time in 1975. He had come out in August of the previous year. He heard about the Belmont Rocks from friends who lived in the city. "That summer was when I first went to the Rocks. What I had heard was, the Rocks were the place where gay people congregated in the summer. The first time I went, I was alone, and I remember being worried that the cars could see me from Lake Shore Drive, so I went to the top tier of rocks, which seemed less conspicuous.

"After that first time, I went there with friends. Sometimes we came into town from Aurora. We knew someone with an apartment in the city. We would meet with friends about twenty feet or so from the statue at the southern end of the Rocks near the gun club. Other groups would do things like bring flags or clusters of balloons to let their group know where they were."

Huberty eventually moved into the city in 1979. "The Belmont Rocks was especially the big place to be on Sundays because later in the afternoon, you would go to the big tea dances in the area. That was such a good time. At the time, the Bushes [3320 N. Halsted] and Crystal's Blinkers [3153 N. Broadway] with the upstairs deck, had the best tea dances.

"I loved walking the Rocks and looking at the paintings," added Huberty. "They were all at different levels of ages. Some that had been there for years were fading, and the new ones were more vibrant. It was interesting to walk along and see the new ones appear while the old ones faded away.

"I remember taking LSD and staying at the Rocks all night, then watching the sunrise over the lake. That sunrise was intense and brilliant; with so many colors, it was completely overwhelming and confusing. Was it just the sunrise?"

Huberty said that sometimes he took a day off work during the week and went to the Rocks. "It was such a peaceful place for me. I would take my light green Fuji racer bike and go down to the Rocks with my Walkman, sit there with my headphones on, and look out at the water. That was a very peaceful place for me. I felt comfortable there. I felt safe there."

❖ ❖ ❖

Victor and Steve at the Belmont Rocks, 1987, from the author's collection.

Jack Delaney was a frequent visitor to the Belmont Rocks between 1975 and 1981. "I worked during the week, but every nice weekend day that I was in town, I would be out there. I would usually be there from 10 a.m. to 2 p.m. I was there to get a suntan. Being there was nice, though. There were friends there, and all you had to do was set down your towel and enjoy all the men in Speedos and the gossip and just being around so many gay people. Some of us were good friends. Then we would go home, take a rest, and get ready to go partying in the evening, usually at the Bushes. I worked at the Bushes part-time, so I drank for free. Sometimes we went to the Closet [3325 N. Broadway] or Broadway Limited [3132 N. Broadway], or Crystal's Blinkers too.

"The Rocks was a great place to meet new people, and even get to play with some of them," adds Delaney. "Back then, things were less open; besides the bars, there weren't a lot of places to meet. Not a lot of organizations were around back then. There just weren't places to socialize in a relaxed environment—but you could do that at the Rocks, and that was what made them so special."

❖ ❖ ❖

Dallas flashes an inviting smile at the Belmont Rocks, 1989, from the author's collection.

"Probably 1976 was when I went to the Belmont Rocks for the first time," said Dallas Bolan. "I was living at Lake Point Towers and think I heard about it from my neighbors across the hall. In those days, I was young, and I soaked everything up like a sponge.

"A friend had a boat that he docked in the harbor, and on Sundays, we would go to brunch and then out on the boat. I remember driving the boat and taking it near the Belmont Rocks, and all the guys got up and were waving and cheering. You couldn't go too close to the Rocks, but that experience of seeing everyone like that showed the congenial sense that was there. The Rocks was like a friendly gay bar, except everyone was in bathing suits."

Bolan added that it was his first experience of seeing such a multitude of gay people all together in the sun. "And everyone was partying and soaking up the sun and celebrating life. That sense of camaraderie and humanity, being caring and non-judgmental, that is all kind of the apex of how I think people should be with one another."

Cotillion on the Rocks
By Rick Karlin, 2018

When I first came out in the late 1970s, I volunteered at Horizons (the LGBT social services agency precursor to the Center on Halsted). I immediately hit it off with a few other volunteers. Ben, Kelvin, and Paul became my closest circle of friends in the community. In the early 1980s, everyone was talking about the best-seller, *The Preppy Handbook*. The preppy style was what many wore: an Izod shirt and a sweater thrown over your shoulders, and a pair of skin-tight designer jeans or pleated linen pants. Although we were as much victims of the fashions of the 1980s as anyone, we also ridiculed the obsession with the preppy lifestyle.

We started calling each other preppy nicknames; Paul was dubbed Muffy Escriva of Southampton, Ben (a librarian) was Cookie, aka Charlotte Webb, of the Webbs of Boston, Peaches Welborne, and I was Helen Highwater MD (Madcap Debutante), of New York, Paris, London, and the World! Somehow, all this evolved into our forming an imaginary group, sort of like the

Junior League, which we called Debutantes Incorporated to Save Humanity (or DISH). We eventually added a "ladies' group" for our female friends, Girls or Females Incorporated to Save Humanity, or GoFISH.

Like most men in our 20s and 30s, we spent most weekends sun-bathing (and cruising) at the Rocks. Whiling the time away, we'd talk about many things: men, fashion, men, politics, men we loved, men we hated, men who'd done us wrong. But whenever we discussed something going on with our little group, we'd always refer to DISH.

As time went on, we added more friends to our circle, but never gave them DISH names. We were trying to decide what to do one Memorial Day and, since it was a particularly warm May, a picnic at the Rocks was in order. We decided that at the picnic, we would officially induct some friends into DISH with a ceremony of some kind. We announced the first "Cotillion on the Rocks."

Because we never did things halfway (does any group of gay men?), we wrote out proclamations, bought rhinestone tiaras and a scepter. We made up both "family names" and preppy monikers for each of them, and each was personalized. One friend was of French heritage, so he was declared "Sabine Rousseau of Paris and Fond du Lac, aka Frenchie." There was also Kiki Murjani, Frances "Cissy" Franklin, and others who have been lost to the recesses of my memory.

We held our induction ceremony on the Rocks, complete with a reading of a proclamation, the inductees taking the DISH pledge, and then being "crowned" with their tiara. Of course, we gathered quite a crowd of onlookers, and the ceremony received a round of applause. We repeated the ceremony for a few years until our core group went our separate ways. Remarkably, many of us made it through the AIDS crisis, but now, there are few of us still alive, which makes me cherish those memories even more."

At a 1976 photo shoot for Gay Chicago *at the Belmont Rocks with paper's publisher, Ralph Paul Gernhardt, in a sleeved T-shirt. Photo by* Gay Chicago *courtesy of the Legacy Project.*

In *States of Desire*, the travel and sex memoir by the late Edmund White (1940-2025) about gay ways and places for getting it on throughout the US, White wrote of visiting the Belmont Rocks in the late 1970s. "The Belmont Rocks are a gay cruising spot. One strolls past an al fresco chess pavilion and a lakeside rifle range and comes upon broad cement steps descending into the water. Here men in trunks or thongs mingle with those in full business regalia; this strange confluence of the underdressed and the overdressed on rocks halfway between the water and eight lanes of speeding traffic turns Chicago by summer into the Rio of North America." (*States of Desire*. White. E.P. Dutton Publishers, 1980).

Steve Stinson also shared a favorite memory of the Belmont Rocks. "Every Saturday and/or Sunday during summer, my best friend and drinking buddy

Dewitt, who lived a few blocks away in Lakeview, would call me in the morning before I had dragged myself out of bed after a late night at the bars. After several irritating rings, I would put the phone to my ear. Before I could mumble a single sound, this piercing voice would shout, "Kick that trick out of bed, and let's go to the Rocks!!!!"

As an avid jogger, the late Dennis Scheibel would often stop at the Belmont Rocks, the Bushes, or the Lincoln Park Lagoon, calling it 'the Trinity of Sleaze.' "It was my incentive to exercise on warm summer evenings. Around 10 p.m. was when the cruising began in earnest, and if you could manage to dodge the police sweeping through with their squad cars at 11 p.m., shining their spotlights and blaring their bullhorns with snarky announcements like, 'The park is now closed, ladies, please exit the park.' [If you dodged that] you could participate in some serious debauchery.

"Sit on the upper level of rocks to announce your arrival. Sit on the lower rocks with your dick out to announce what you were there for. Sometimes, if there was already action going on, you could be invited to join in or watch. Sometimes, you were 'dismissed' to move along. You couldn't take these rejections too seriously...

"The Rocks had a chain link fence that divided the area, and if you and your trick(s) were brave enough to hold onto the fence and swing yourselves out over the Lake water onto the other side, you could have a more "private" encounter...

"...At times, the thought of what was going on all around, while clueless Lake Shore Drive traffic and straight people out for evening walks, jogs, and bike rides were all around, it made me feel that I was part of an exclusive, secret club. I had to be cautious about who I spoke to about it lest it all disappear. I guess that's what happened. Too many talked about it. The city swooped in. The Rocks became a revetment project. The horny boys went online. The end of an era." (Dennis Scheibel, 2018. RIP Dennis (1952-2021).

David Plambeck joined the Windy City LGBT Bowling League in 1979. Bowling for a gay team, he quickly met other people. Then he joined the Horizons gay youth group and began playing 16-inch softball for the bar His n' Hers [944 W. Addison]. Prior to joining the softball league, Plambeck had never been to the Belmont Rocks. Softball practice for the His 'n Hers team was on Wednesday nights at the Rocks. "We practiced just beyond the parking lot."

Several years later, Plambeck lived for a while on Aldine and then on Barry, so the Rocks were very close by. "I frequently rode my bike there carrying a towel, Sun-In for my hair, a cassette player with recent disco tunes, and a spray bottle filled with water to cool me off.

"There were those huge boulders," Plambeck added, recalling that he was fearful of entering the water. "The water was so cold, and I didn't know the depth and didn't want to step on a broken beer bottle or anything like that.

"I never met anyone there, never experienced doing drugs there." He described the Rocks as "relaxing, tranquil, and peaceful." After typically two hours or so in the sun, Plambeck would collect his things and pedal back home.

Love at the Belmont Rocks. Photo by Gay Chicago *courtesy of the Legacy Project.*

Growing up in Chicago, Steve Kimbrough heard about the Rocks when he was still in high school. "I went there for the first time with my friend Ray in 1978 or 1979. He would pick me up in his car. We went there three or four times that summer. We couldn't get into bars, and there was nowhere to meet gay people.

"At the Rocks, I felt like I could be myself and not feel out of place," said Kimbrough. "That was also when I realized how many other gay people were around—and there were lots of them. We sat there and watched the guys lying around on the grass and on the rocks in hardly any clothing. At the time, I had a thing for hairy chests, and there was plenty of that on display.

"The Rocks was a place you could be yourself, and for me at the time that meant a place where you weren't going to get hassled, a place where you could smoke pot, have sex, and get drunk too. What more could you want?"

When Kimbrough eventually moved into the neighborhood, the lawn at the Belmont Rocks was a favorite place to have a barbecue. "We did it regularly. There were usually about six of us, everybody would bring something, and we would just spend the day barbecuing and drinking, smoking and having fun."

❖ ❖ ❖

In the southern storefront of what is now Unabridged Bookstore (3251 N. Broadway) was the clothing and 'whatnot' store, Stuff 'n Such. The store was primarily filled with gay fashions of the era. According to a 1977 advertisement

Stuff 'n Such, a clothing store on Broadway near Melrose offering "fashions for the Belmont Rocks."

in *Gay Life,* "Stuff 'n Such carried 'Jeans. Tops. Fatigue shorts. Rain wear. Navy Whites. Web belts and God knows what all." Instead of beachwear, Stuff 'n' Such carried "Fashions for the Belmont Rocks!!"

"When I was at the Bistro," offered TL Noble, "in probably 1976 or 1977, Eddie Dugan [the Bistro owner] knew a guy who came in the bar named Michael who was a boat captain. Eddie ended up buying a 22-foot Chris-Craft boat with Captain Mike as the captain. Sometimes in the summer, Eddie would have Captain Mike go get the boat from Belmont Harbor and bring it downtown to the river by the Bistro [420 N. Dearborn], and then we would go down there and get on board. Sometimes we did that three or four nights a week after the Bistro closed. We would take the boat out and anchor off the Belmont Rocks.

"Once we went into a cave. You had to go underwater to get there, so we took a bunch of tea lights in Ziploc bags and some booze. Any drugs we did, we did at the bar or on the boat there. That night, when we went inside, there were six of us. The cave was large, twenty feet long and eight feet wide, maybe five feet high. There were ledges inside the cave where you could sit, and we had tea lights on the ledges. We stayed in there and partied until the sun came up. When we came out, it was early morning, and there were people there who I am sure were watching us come out from that cave and thinking, 'Where are all these people coming from?'"

Paul Mikos first visited the Rocks in June 1976. He had graduated from high school the previous year. "I had a friend in the city, Roy, who was more versed in gay life. He invited me to the Rocks one day. I didn't know what to expect.

"It was like a carnival with primarily men hanging out on all the rugged and ragged rocks. What struck me most was the sheer number of people, like me, uninhibited and free. After we spent the day, he took me to my first gay bar, Shari's [2901 N. Clark]. For a while, you could drink beer and wine in Illinois at 19."

Mikos continued, "In the summer, people went to the Rocks at all hours, skinny dipping day and night. I remember the sound of shots over the lake from the gun club. The art on the Rocks early on was more hippie style—flowers, hearts, and all that sort of thing. AIDS changed the artwork there, and it became a place of memorial.

"I remember listening to the latest disco hits on everyone's boom box, and in those days at the Rocks everyone had their dial tuned to WDAI, all disco. At dusk, guys would slip over into the gun club after it closed and carry on. During the day, people would have floaties and inflatable donuts and would tie them together in flotillas. There were picnics. There was partying.

"All the days there blended," laughed Mikos. "The Rocks was very much a community hangout and social scene with lots of cruising. But I remember it more as a big outside party. In the 1970s, the bars still felt risky, and it felt safe there. In my late teens and early twenties, I went there on the weekends and sometimes during the week. I would meet friends there, which was a big deal before cellphones. We would call and say, 'We will be there at noon, south end of the Rocks, on a big yellow blanket.' We'd meet up like that. There was nothing like it."

Vera Washington probably first went to the Belmont Rocks in 1978 or 1979. "I had heard people talking about these Rocks and I didn't know what they meant. It was finally a girlfriend who took me there for the first time. It was nice. I started going there, mostly on Sundays. That was part of our ritual on the weekends. I also took my children when I went there, and they were about seven and nine at the time. We would sit around and barbecue and interact and walk the park and jump rope, which was big at the time, and listen to music and just have a nice time in the park.

"Groups of us congregated by the parking lot and then moved into the grass. Eventually, I started going up on the Rocks with my blanket and my champagne. I miss the Rocks, the openness, and the freedom of it. Sometimes we went there and saw the sunset. It was just a place to enjoy life."

Washington added, "Even now, when I drive down Lake Shore Drive, I always look over; it's nice over there, but we are not there. As I often say to young people today, you all don't know what you all missed."

Marshall Titus first heard about the Rocks in the late 1970s. "At the time, the idea of going to the North Side was like going to a different country on so many levels. Being Black and going to the North Side was a scary thought, especially when you put being gay on top of that.

"I first went to the Belmont Rocks probably around 1982 and found out it was about being there and hanging out and enjoying the lake, and the freedom to be whatever. Everybody was out there, and it was such a good vibe. People just enjoying the area and not feeling restricted."

After his first time at the Rocks, Titus returned, but since he was still living a good distance away in Hyde Park, his commutes to the Rocks were rare. "But once I moved into the neighborhood in 1999, I went there all the time to chill, enjoy the lake, and people-watch. The Rocks usually had some real characters around. I thought the idea of the After Pride party was cool, but personally, I always liked the Rocks when there were fewer people there, but that's the introvert in me. The Rocks was its own universe. I was sad when they eventually put up the barriers around it."

The late 1980s, Ted on the lawn at the Belmont Rocks. Photo courtesy of Marty Hyams.

Daniel Layman knew about the Belmont Rocks long before he went there. "My dad grew up near there." Layman shared that his father had moved into the area in 1928, when he was six years old. His dad lived first at Broadway and Waveland and then at Seminary and Diversey. His father remained in the area until after high school. Daniel had heard of the Belmont Rocks, but never as a gay beach. "My father and uncles even called them the Belmont Rocks."

Years later, David experienced the Belmont Rocks for himself. "I spent time at the Belmont Rocks during my junior and senior years in college at DePaul

University, 1980-1982. A few times when I was taking a summer semester course, I think I even brought a tax accounting textbook with me to the Rocks to study. After classes in the summer or on summer days with no classes, I usually ventured to the Rocks, where I could look at beautiful men lounging, and gasp at the braver ones swimming, and some even jumping off the rocks there.

"Gay guys seemed to come and leave the rocks in several waves. The early arrivals left around 4 p.m., some going to jobs as waiters. Another group arrived about that time, perhaps having left work early to get a little sun. Others were there all the time—several told me they were teachers with months of the summer off, allowing them to spend many days at the Rocks... "

Layman was about 20 when he met his best friend, Jim, and another friend, Sean, at the gay bar, Alfie's [900 N. Rush Street]. "One Friday night at Alfie's, Sean suggested that, when he finished his shift, we drive up to the Belmont Rocks. I waited around for Sean to finish his night shift. Sean informed me that a regular gaggle of gays ended up at the Rocks in the early dawn to smoke pot or do some last-ditch cruising after the bars closed.

"That early morning when Sean and I went to the Rocks was, in fact, my very first time ever smoking pot. Smoking weed did not happen at my regimented boarding high school, and I had never tried it before that night at the Belmont Rocks. In those days, I was a serious and politically conservative student with professional plans, despite my wanton roaming through Chicago's gay underworld during my college years.

"Sean, Jim, and I, and another pal piled into my Honda Civic and went to the Belmont Rocks that Friday night/early Saturday morning. Sean, with his arm in a cast, apparently had a greater affinity and more experience than I with pot smoking. After a while at the Belmont Rocks, Sean began telling us about the cool caverns he had explored under the rocks, which he had figured out how to swim into. With courage bolstered from the pot, or just to show off, Sean, with his arm in a cast, slid off a rock and swam into one of the caves. It seemed forever until he came back out, and I honestly thought we might never see him alive again. It would be years later that I learned that the caverns under Rocks were remnants of the days when the US government Nike missile silos were positioned there.

"I finished college, went to graduate school, and joined a large Chicago firm, and my days of going to the Belmont Rocks largely ended, except for regular bike rides past the area after work and on weekends. I learned while doing historical research a few years ago that the grassy area around the Belmont Rocks was Chicago's original north lakefront golf course, before landfill extended Lincoln Park northward and the much larger Waveland/ Sydney R. Marovitz Golf Course opened."

Now married and partnered with his husband of over twenty years, Layman lives in retirement in Florida. "Those memories of youth and adventure and exploration, including days and nights at the Belmont Rocks, contributed to my self-discovery and to my becoming a proud gay man. Those memories are still very special, and they sometimes seem like only yesterday."

In "On the Rocks," a 1980 feature in the *Chicago Reader*, Marcia Froelke Coburn wrote, "All the ingredients for a hot Saturday at the rocks are present. The sunshine is relentless, the lake surprisingly clear, and hundreds of male bodies, displayed to within an inch of public decency, are waiting to be admired. The flaunting of flesh and the need to be admired are the two staples that have made the Belmont Rocks, as *Gay Chicago* publisher Ralph Paul says, '*the* gay beach in Chicago.'

"Actually, the name Belmont Rocks is a misnomer. The gay area is a barren stretch that starts where Wellington Street would intersect with the lake and runs south to the Park District statue of a nuclear American Indian family. Nor is the term 'beach' entirely correct. There is no sand, just grass (constantly soggy from a broken water main) and tiers of limestone rocks. Swimming is not officially sanctioned by the Park District. ('It's a hazardous area with a lot of underwater debris,' says Joseph Pecorara, Chicago Park District general supervisor of beaches and pools. 'We will not guard any area that's not absolutely safe because if you put a lifeguard there, then people are going to assume they can go in the water.'

"...Although some older homosexuals remember the Belmont Rocks as a predominantly gay beach in the early 1940s (and the Gay and Lesbian History Project turned up a gay man who joined others there in the late 1930s), most Chicago gays agree that the rocks were not established gay territory until the early 1960s...

"...It is perfect suntan weather, clear and warm with a slight breeze off the lake. Jeff says he knows it, and he will shut up and lie down for a minute, but first, he wants to explain a few things.

"This is a beach for *men*," he says. "The gay section of the Oak Street beach?" He wrinkles his nose in disgust. 'That's for kids, gay babies.'

"...'I've come here for 11 years,' he says, 'I practically came out on the rocks. I've made friends here, found and lost lovers, and had the best summers of my life here.'

"Because of his experience, Jeff considers himself something of an authority on the local customs and on, as he puts it, 'the *je ne sais quoi* of the place.' Throughout my several weeks of hanging out at the rocks, Jeff is happy to share any information he considers useful.

"'See, everyone here has his own rock, his own claim to the territory. It's *his rock*,' he smacks his palm on the limestone, 'and you'll find him there every time.'

"'So this is your rock.'

"'Well, actually, somebody's sitting on my rock today. But you can always find me in this general area.'

"'This general area' is the southern and most heavily populated end of the rocks. The appeal of the southern end lies, in part, in the chance to swim. Although underwater rocks border the entire stretch on the shoreline south of the Belmont Harbor, swimming at the southern end is far safer than at the northern, where, every year, in spite of freshly stenciled Park District warnings, people jump in and break bones. ...

"'This is the best place to sit,' Jeff continued. 'It's open, friendly, relaxed. Not like the lawn at all.' He waves a hand at the neighboring grassy park. 'Everybody over there is a social butterfly. 'Who went to what party? Who's hot? Who's not? Who makes the best pastry *brisee*? It's a bunch of queens over there.'

"Jeff is a little less disdainful about the northern end of the rocks. 'You should go up there and then talk to the queens on the lawn, but you'll end up back here. I always have—for 11 summers.'

"...On the lawn, Brian is sitting in the shade of a beach umbrella...'Brian says he is a lawyer, and he seems to feel that this information refutes Jeff's charge that 'only queens sit on the lawn.' He has a baby-doll face and a polished, almost courtly manner. He is 32 years old and has been coming to the rocks for about seven years.

"At first it was a very important part of my life; beyond wanting to be here, I felt this need. Sometimes during the week, I'd call in sick at work and then spend the day there. I never do that now, but I was younger then [and] had this—oh, I don't know, this feeling that this was what life was; this illusion of perfect permanent summer.'

"Roger agrees, 'We all literally live here during the day. One guy named Joe even set up his own concession stand. He'd lug ice and soda and even a hibachi for hamburgers over here. The cops were always trying to catch him selling stuff, but Joe would say it was a party, and everyone backed him up. It felt that way. Then one day, the cops were back checking and some dizzy queen yelled, 'How much for the Coke?' That blew it. ..." (Coburn, 'On the Rocks,' *The Chicago Reader*, September 12, 1980. V9, #50].

In the late 1970s, David Zak was teaching in the suburbs when he fell madly in love, quit his teaching job, and in 1979, he moved to the city. "Michael and I moved into a place across from Illinois Masonic. We were in the neighborhood, so we spent a lot of time at the Rocks. They were not beautiful, but they were ours. Michael was a very social and fun-loving guy. We had lots of good times there, lots of fun times, and frisky times, at least for then.

"Michael Hansen was his name," added Zak. "He was cast in the first touring production of *Evita*. That was sort of the end of our relationship. He toured with that, and his residence became mainly New York after that. Around 1983, Michael was back in town and asked me to meet him at the Rocks. He said he had something to tell me. That day was the first time I had someone say, right to my face, that they had AIDS.

"The Rocks was a fun place, it was an amazing experience with the music and the camaraderie and all that, but because of that conversation with Michael, the place has a sadness for me as well. Michael died in 1985, when he was 29 and I was 30."

❖ ❖ ❖

Chen Ooi went to the Belmont Rocks for the first time in 1979, shortly after he met Bill [Kelley]. "He took me there. I had never experienced anything like the Rocks. I remember we sat on the embankment and watched the men. Some were naked, but nothing was going on. That kind of thing happened at night. That was when there was more cruising and things going on, especially when there used to be bushes and trees there, but those were cut down sometime in the 1980s."

❖ ❖ ❖

A very weekend day at the Belmont Rocks from the 1980s. Photo courtesy of David Klein.

❖ ❖ ❖

"I used to cruise and pick up guys in the 1970s and 1980s by walking along the lagoon, and I ended up going to the Rocks from there," shared Mrkt. "I usually picked someone up and we went back to my place. Sometimes I had sex in the bushes, but not usually, and sometimes I had sex at the Rocks in the places closer to the water. I used to be a big bike rider, and the Rocks were where I ended my ride.

"Sex was a big part of going there at first," said Mrkt, "but I ended up meeting three of the six soul mates I've known in my life at the Belmont Rocks—all three of them were great friends.

"The Rocks were a place where you could go and socialize, a lot of that. It became a destination with friends or a place I could go and find friends. I am not a big sun person, but for a while I lived across the street on Briar. It was so convenient; if I felt like hanging out with people, the Rocks were right across the street. Friends of mine had a standing invitation to meet there on weekends in the afternoon. People would come and go. It was always loose. Even if you wandered over during the week or anytime, the Rocks was a place where it was almost impossible not to know at least a few people.

"The Rocks were social and cruisy during the day, but at night, it seemed like it was almost all cruising and sex over there. I used to walk over there at night and on the lawn after the park closed. There would be lots of guys out there on the prowl for sex. You had to be careful," added Mrkt. "Not just from getting busted. But there were bashers out there too. You had to be very aware. I couple of my friends got mugged there. Some guys also went down onto the Rocks at night to mess around, but I didn't trust going down those blocks in the dark."

In 1979, Joe Knell was a 19-year-old college student at school in Champaign, IL. One day, he decided to take the Amtrak to Chicago. "I wasn't going to get a hotel room. I planned to just meet someone when I went out. I came up with my fake ID—so I was Kevin O'Hara for the day.

"I went to one of the gay bars down in the River North area, or whatever River North was called then. My plan worked. I met someone and I stayed the night at his place. The next day, he loaned me some swim trunks, since I had only come to Chicago with the clothes I'd worn, and then he took me to the Rocks. There were gay men everywhere. We hung out there all afternoon. I think I spent a second night with him as well. He was a nice guy. Sweet. Handsome."

Five years later, when Knell returned to Chicago, things were different. "By then, I was into new wave music, and so being tan wasn't exactly a priority. Being pale was better. By then, I was going to places like Berlin [954 W. Belmont], Dolores and Eddie's [3700 N. Broadway], and the Orbit Room [3708 N. Broadway]. But we would still go to the Rocks and sit sometimes and talk. Then we would inevitably see people and sit down and talk with them.

"Sometimes I would go to the Rocks by myself," continued Knell. "There was something about sitting there and looking out at the lake that was so calming. There's something soothing about a large body of water. I found it a comfort even in winter."

❖ ❖ ❖

Late 1980s. Bar picnic for the Closet (3325 N. Broadway) at the Belmont Rocks. The author is holding up a Frisbee.

Peter Tuthill was still drinking back in 1983. At the time, he had been living with his partner, Alex Prentzas, for a while. "One afternoon, I decided to go to the Belmont Rocks to get some sun, so I dragged my lawn chair out there as well as a six-pack. Drinking the six-pack in the sun, I got drunk. Then I took my suit off and put it over my lap...and then I passed out. I was awakened as sunset approached by two Chicago police officers. So, I am standing there

1990. Peter enjoying the day at the Belmont Rocks. Photo courtesy of Neil.

trying to put my bathing suit on and asking them what the problem is. They took me in a paddy wagon to Town Hall at Halsted and Addison and put me in a holding tank. It was, 'faggot this' and 'faggot that,' but eventually I fell asleep in the cell. Meanwhile, Alex had no idea where I was and was terribly worried. The next morning at 10 a.m., the cop came in and said, 'Ok, your time is up.' The police officer who escorted me out of the station turned to me and said, 'They really messed with you.' Then, as I was leaving the station, I saw Alex running down Halsted. He was roaming the streets trying to find me. And we ran towards one another just like in a movie. That was my most memorable time there."

Tuthill went to the Belmont Rocks for the first time a few years before meeting Alex. "I moved to Chicago in 1978, and I had heard about the Rocks from the people I had met here. I came to Chicago from Virginia by the Atlantic Ocean, so the whole idea of a beach on a lake was bizarre. I had seen lakes, but never this big. And I had never seen a beach like this.

"I was living on Melrose, so I started going there in the summer of 1979 and went there quite a bit. I always went to the Rocks alone, but the Rocks was also a great place to be social. There was a good amount of drinking, and sometimes there was marijuana in the air as well. You could do that if you wanted. You could go to tan or cruise or pick up a trick on occasion, though I never tricked at the Belmont Rocks."

"The first time I went to the Rocks was probably when I moved to Belmont and Sheridan in 1979," said Tuthill's partner, Alex Prentzas. "I was going to Northwestern. Someone told me the cruisy places around were the Lincoln Park bushes and lagoon, and the Belmont Rocks. So I went to the Belmont Rocks, and truthfully, I was coming from Greece. I thought, 'This is not a beach, it's just a bunch of uncomfortable rocks.' Then my libido started to take over when I noticed all the cute men.

"I remember going there once, and for some reason the She Devils were square dancing there in women's swimwear with wigs and their elaborate heavy makeup, which was melting down their faces in the heat and humidity. Then a couple of other drag queens who were in the park joined them, and then a third. Everyone was just high and having fun.

"Peter and I hung out there all the time," added Prentzas. "We went there probably two times a week in the summer. We would sit there and talk to friends, lie in the sun, and sometimes get high. I have such fond memories of the place. But mostly because it was the place where Peter and I met."

Greg McFall recalled the 1970s at the Belmont Rocks. "It was the place to go to skinny dip and sunbathe nude. Approaching the Rocks, it looked like a bunch of campsites. People gathered in their groups and set up camp. Some groups would go all out in how they set up their camp. Others would just spread out their towels together. The lawn was colorful and decorative with all the groups." McFall added, "Many of the Rocks themselves were decorated with art and were colorful. The best way to describe the Rocks was that it looked like a festival."

1985. The lawn area on a sunny day at the Belmont Rocks. On summer weekends the green was packed. Photo courtesy of Norman Shimkus.

"A bunch of us gay guys would gather by the Rocks on Tuesday evenings during the summer to play a pickup game of 16-inch softball," recalled Pat Riley. "We played on a field that we laid out ourselves just south and east of the southernmost parking lot, east of Lake Shore Drive, with the actual Rocks located to the east, just beyond our Left Field space. It was first-come, first-pick on which position to play. You would just sign up on a sheet of paper and write down your position. Left Field and Shortstop always filled up first."

Riley also shared that afterwards, one of the participants in the game would host a meal in his home, or maybe outside. "He would have lots of help. We would all contribute a small amount, I think two or three dollars."

The Lincoln Park Lagooners was one of Chicago's first gay and lesbian social organizations. Though incorporated in 1977, the Lagooners had already been around for several years. At its peak, the group had hundreds of members.

The origins of the Lagooners can be traced to a few gay volleyball players who met regularly at Lincoln Park's North Pond, aka "the lagoon." The group focused on social interaction, camaraderie, and friendship outside of the bars.

This was achieved through organized activities—camping trips, softball games, movie nights, bowling, volleyball, winter ski trips, summer rafting trips, game nights, and holiday parties.

Another aspect of the Lagooners was their commitment to give back to the community. To accomplish this, the Lagooners held massive charity events. Thousands attended their shindigs at the Aragon Ballroom [1106 W. Lawrence] and the Broadway Armory [5917 N. Broadway]—theme parties with names like Cruisin' the Nile and Tropical Lei. These fundraisers were some of the first of their kind in Chicago's gay community and helped to serve as templates for many of the large-scale AIDS galas that were to come in the 1980s and 1990s.

The Lincoln Park Lagooners eventually disbanded in 2016. (The Chicago LGBT Hall of Fame)

❖ ❖ ❖

Chicago gay pioneer Bob Gammie and the Lincoln Park
Lagooners were instrumental in the continued popularity of the
Belmont Rocks as a gathering place for LGBT Chicagoans.
Photo courtesy of F. Nichter

Bob Gammie (1925-2014) was the heart and soul of the Lincoln Park Lagooners. His 2014 *Windy City Times* obituary reads, "Known as 'Ma' or 'Gammie' among his many friends, he was active in the community for more than 60 years. Gammie moved to Chicago in 1949, and during the 1950s and 1960s, he organized social gatherings—including weekly Tuesday night barbecues, softball games that later morphed into Chicago's gay softball leagues, bowling and volleyball games—that evolved into the Lincoln Park Lagooners, Chicagoland's first gay and lesbian social organization."

In the obituary, longtime friend Greg Neil said, "Bob always said 'life is a party' and he was 'the hostess with the mostest.' He had so much energy, and we all fed off of it. It was contagious. He acquired the nickname 'Ma' because he was a den mother to so many younger gay men like myself. I also lived in his home [5333 N. Lakewood], which he called the Winter Palace. It was so refreshing for me to see Bob live as an openly gay man long before anyone was talking about gay rights." ("Longtime leader and activist Bob Gammie dies." Carrie Maxwell, *Windy City Times*, February 2, 2014).

The men of the Belmont Rocks. Photo courtesy of Paul Kubek.

In 1982, Dan Berger moved into Lakeview. "My friend Brent was the one who first took me to the Belmont Rocks. After that, my friends and I would go there on weekends and sometimes at night during the week to have a few beers or skinny dip. The Rocks was a safe space to be with the community, where we were free to show affection or intimacy, and no one really interfered.

"The Rocks were in the middle of Chicago and near Lake Shore Drive and yet felt very safe and secluded. The Rocks felt like home. Everyone there seemed to be in relaxation mode, and there was much camaraderie and friendship."

Some of Berger's friends, usually a group of about six, would meet at the Rocks, and those friends would sometimes bring others along. "The group grew that way. Once a friend brought a guy he had tricked with the night before, and it turned out that I had tricked with the guy the night before that—but we all had fun with it. At the Rocks, there was a lot of joking and fun. They were a mainstay of the whole gay scene. There was no place like it."

"My summer at the Belmont Rocks was the summer of 1981," said Bob Wilson, who was in a relationship and living on the North Side when he first heard about the gay beach. "Gary was a few years older, and one day he just matter-of-factly said, 'Let's go to the Rocks.' We had a place in Uptown at the time, so we took the train down to Belmont with all our beach gear and were walking toward the lake and as we got closer there was one of those big old brownstones and the front door was wide open and blaring from inside was Diana Ross and whoever was singing Diana was taking the lead in the song. Gary turned to me and said, 'We're getting close.'

"Going there for the first time was amazing. A totally gay world...I almost get the image of Dorothy as she steps into Oz. The Rocks were on levels going down, like a theater, down from ground level. It was magical to be there with your people and the lake in that secluded place, really like a secret cove. I could not believe I had been riding my bike past this place for a year. I never caught on, but it was down like that and away from the bike path.

"I had never seen a mass of gay people in the daylight before. I had never been to a Pride Parade. The only groups of gay people I had seen were in a bar, and then you would never see everyone—the dance boys had their bars, the women had their bars, and the leathermen went to their places. At the Rocks, there was a mix of everybody.

"I could not believe there was a spot where I could lie out on my towel right beside my boyfriend. Or that we could lie there holding hands, and we did. Or cuddle with him or kiss him. We could never do that anywhere else. At the Rocks, you were safe. You were with comrades.

"I probably went to the Rocks a half dozen times that summer. Bicycling down. Nothing but laughter, eating, sunning, smoking weed...the music was going on different boom boxes. The Rocks were a joyous experience."

The following spring, Wilson moved to California, returning in the winter of 2004/2005. "My mom was ill and living on Aldine. I was home to help care for her. The first Saturday I was home, it was probably ten degrees out. That didn't matter—I walked down to the Rocks. I had heard the city had changed a lot along the lakefront. I went down there that day and walked around, trying to find them. I kept checking my memory. Weren't the Rocks right here? Maybe they are further ahead... Finally, I realized the Rocks were gone. I never imagined they would be part of the lakefront changes. At that moment, I was hit with overwhelming sadness, remembering that summer. Losing the Rocks was like losing a part of that, and like an erasure of that summer."

❖ ❖ ❖

Testing the water at the Belmont Rocks, from the author's collection.

Merri Monks first went to the Belmont Rocks in the late 1970s. "It was the stretch of lakefront that no one else wanted, and so we took it over. I lived on Halsted and Barry, and I used to go there on weekends before I got sober in 1986."

After getting sober, Monks called the Belmont Rocks a life-changing place. "Four of us lesbians from New Town Alano Club [909 W. Belmont], a couple, and then another friend would go there. It was a safe place to hang out. I remember going to the Rocks and enjoying the company, even if I didn't know a lot of the people, I enjoyed being in the presence of all these people being themselves and being okay to be myself too. Just sitting out on the Rocks was a pleasure. It was a wonderful daytime place, a safe outdoor space where we didn't have to spend money. The Rocks were a nice gay alternative to bar life."

❖ ❖ ❖

The treacherous shoreline of the Belmont Rocks. Photo from the author's collection.

❖ ❖ ❖

Man drowns at Belmont Rocks
by Paul Cotton

"A man not yet positively identified drowned July 16 at the Belmont Rocks, a popular gay sunning area on the lakefront between Belmont Avenue and Diversey Parkway.

"The 25-35-year-old black man was wearing only swim trunks, according to the 23rd (Town Hall) district police. A spokesperson for the Cook County medical examiner's office said a friend of the victim came in with a name but no address and few other details. Police are trying to locate family members to make a positive identification.

"A witness said the man dived into Lake Michigan shortly after noon and disappeared. Swimming at the rocks is common, despite the 'no swimming, no diving' signs...." (*Gay Life* newspaper, July 23, 1982).

Gary Preston was looking to leave St. Louis and visited Chicago to see what sort of place it would be to live. "The first person I came out to in college had moved here, and she urged me to come see the city. She was a straight woman, but she saw the gay community all around in Chicago. So, I visited. I had another friend with me, and he had heard about the Belmont Rocks, and we decided to go there."

When Preston moved to Chicago in 1981, he settled into a place at Roscoe and Broadway, and the Belmont Rocks were a quick bike ride away. "I went there all the time. It was social and sometimes cruisy, but mostly social. I was a sun worshipper, and I loved being tan. I was new to Chicago, and I wanted to make new friends—and I did, I made a lot of friends there. We would meet and lie out together. The Rocks were a place to be social during the day. We would go and smoke pot, gossip, look at boys, and meet people. We preferred the grass. It was more comfortable.

"When I gathered my courage, I climbed down the slimy rocks and into the lake. It was very easy to get banged up on the rocks there. You could use a float or a raft at the Rocks; actually, they were not allowed, but the Rocks were never patrolled. I remember the guy with the ice cream cart and those mango and strawberry popsicles."

Preston also recalled a bit of the vernacular. "The word we had for a hot guy was 'squankable' which meant fuckable—that caught on. We were all so young. We would meet out there and make our plans for the evening—the Bistro [420 N. Dearborn], and later Paradise [2848 N. Broadway], or Broadway Limited [3132 N. Broadway]."

Preston added that many of his friends from the Belmont Rocks eventually died of AIDS. "At least half—Wayne, Dan, Jim...Wayne was my best friend. As time went by, people were getting sick and dying. We talked about that at the Rocks as well. Every week, it seemed like we found out someone we knew either had it or had died."

In 1982, Rick Kasprzak moved to Chicago from Wisconsin for his first job out of school. His new place in Chicago was in Lakeview. "I had a cousin who had lived in Lincoln Park for about five years, and she offered to show me around. So, we were going all around seeing the sights and she's saying, this is the Ace Hardware [2818 N. Broadway] where they'll have everything for you, and here is RJ Grunts [2056 N. Lincoln Park W] with the best brunch around, and then we went up Lake Shore Drive and she said, 'Oh and there's the gay beach.' She said it very matter-of-factly. I was very closeted at the time, but I made a note of where this place was. And then she was on to the next thing, saying, 'Those are the tennis courts'... This was probably in February of 1982."

Kasprzak continued, "That spring, maybe in April, we had one of those tease summer days where the weather is warm and sunny. I worked retail at the time, and I had a half day, so I thought, 'I'm going to check out that gay beach.' I was so nervous. I had never been to a gay bar and didn't really know any gay people. So, I took my chair and my towel, and my boom box, and went there, and within an hour, this guy walks up to me and was being very chit-chatty, and finally sat down, and we had a very enjoyable conversation. No talk of gayness or anything. So, I was really confused. We didn't exchange any contact information or anything."

Jim Lawless had recently bought a condo in the 2800 Lake Shore Drive building. "So, the Rocks were right in my backyard." Lawless gave his version of his initial encounter with Kasprzak. "I'm walking along the Rocks and see him in his chaise longue chair. Green nylon shorts, big smile, boom box, and maybe a cooler. He was the cutest thing I had ever seen. I'm older. I was 34 and he was 24. There was an instant attraction between us, and I asked to sit down, and we started talking. I sat there for the next two or three hours, and we just talked about each other and our loves, our gay experiences, and our families.

Everything. Then it was time to go, and I was so mesmerized by him that I forgot to get his phone number. I was kicking myself! In those days, that was the first thing you did! But I lived across the street from the Rocks, so every nice day that I could after that, I went back to the Rocks looking for him. And I guess he was doing sort of the same thing, looking for me."

Kasprzak interjected, "Then maybe a month later, I went back to the Belmont Rocks, and that guy, Jim, was there. We both said it was so good to see each other, and he sat down."

"And there he was," added Lawless. "And we picked up where we left off. For years, we had picnic lunches and dinners there. We had a number of our anniversary picnics at the Rocks."

"We have been together ever since seeing one another again, since the summer of 1982—42 years," said Kasprzak in 2024. "He is still the love of my life. We are so in synch with one another that I can't imagine life with anyone else. We've had a wonderful time growing old together. If you ask him about me, he'll say, 'I thought he was a summer fling, but little did I know I would spend the rest of my life with this guy.'"

Pate Pontiac used to hang out at the Rocks regularly. "With both my girlfriends and boyfriends. In summer, it was just the place to be. One very clear memory of the Rocks was Memorial Day of 1980. I was there with Dolly Kaly, who owned the lesbian bar, the Swan Club [3720 N. Clark], with her partner Anna. Dolly was an older, super-cool lesbian, a friend and a mentor of mine. Dolly was just the best. We always used to sit on the Rocks, but I remember one Memorial Day, it was raining, and we had made our way out there. We were sitting with our coats over our heads in the rain, smoking opium with a couple of other friends. All those sunny days at the Rocks, it's interesting how the rainy day is the most memorable.

"Another time, I was there with Pinky, who used to clean a lot of the bars. We went out there and were smoking a joint. It must have been early morning after the bar closed. We were really high, and we were at the Rocks. From a distance, we see these two huge Dobermans charging towards us across the grass. We looked at the dogs and at each other with this look of, 'What the hell is happening?' Then we screamed and took off, and as we were running, we saw the dogs veer off and go towards some people over on the side.

A lesbian party at the Belmont Rocks circa 1980. The women tended to congregate on the northern edge of the Belmont Rocks while the men were more likely to gravitate towards the southern end. Photos courtesy of Janice Polito.

"A lot of times I would go to the Rocks with six or eight girlfriends and bring a radio and hang out and smoke pot and listen to music. I had some artist friends who would do things there, and they would paint, and we would chat." Pontiac describes this period as 'my first wave of going to the Rocks.'

"My second wave of going to the Rocks was a few years later, when I was hanging out with the punks and the freaks. We would go there at night, and at night, the Rocks were a different animal. You had to be careful to navigate the Rocks carefully. If the moon was out, it was so gorgeous sitting there with the waves crashing and all. Things got a little less safe at night, but we were young punks and feared nothing. We would go there more in the fall than in the summer, when it was cooler outside, and we would go in our leather jackets. We were the creatures of the night. We would sit and laugh and drink and smoke pot. We all worked in bars—Berlin, Limelight [632 N. Dearborn], clubs where it was loud and smoky. This was our fresh air in the middle of the city. We were all good friends. This was our peace and quiet, a much-needed evening of decompression and laughs."

The Rocks: Are You Family?
By Princess Hana

"I called my God brother Micky to clarify the details of when we first discovered 'The Rocks.' It made sense that he would've been with me during that time, and it made sense to call him about that specific time. We came out together, shared all of our 'gay' secrets, and enjoyed the sparkling culture with the harsh realities of being gay black teens in the eighties.

"Oh yeah, it was 1984. I could imagine him blinking his green eyes, that he's still adored for by the gays and most humans. I listened as we recalled the time when somebody told us about the place, and soon after, we took the bus and train all the way there, walking from the Belmont L to the lakefront.

"Remember, Sundays was the shit, especially after 5 p.m., especially for US.

"I knew exactly what he meant. For certain, there were many similarities and differences that drove whites, Black, and Brown folks there. One thing is for sure: it was our sanctuary that belonged to us—all of us!

"I can still see my late teen and young adult self, looking forward to endless summers to be gay and free. It's funny that as a middle-aged, proud same-gender-loving, Black American womxn today, my daily self-care goals is all about liberating myself from titles, unnecessary material things, and being my authentic free self without being 'under the white gaze' as Toni Morrison once taught us.

"What was freedom to me as a 'gay' girl in the backdrop of House music, Michael Jackson, Prince, and the eighties 'gender benders' like Culture Club and Eurythmics? It meant being safe in place and identity. Yes, I grew up in the multicultural, middle-class Hyde Park, which was probably better than many places to explore one's identity. Yet, it was the beginning of the HIV epidemic, and intolerance with violence toward the LGBTQIAA+ communities was coated in shame, stigma, ignorance, verbal attacks, and physical assaults, especially with the gay boys and trans girls. Yes, even on our tree-lined streets and lake views of Hyde Park, we were still gay and black on the South Side. Where was my gay liberation in the eighties and nineties? It was at The Rocks. It was like being sucked into a magical portal the first time my friends and I discovered our queer sanctuary. I'm not sure if we discovered it or if it discovered us, but we uncovered many truths about ourselves with the understanding that there is no one way to be 'gay' or part of the LGBTQIAA+ family that is beautiful and expansive.

"And...

"The lake reflected many colors of our rainbow. It was the place for us to 'pooch,' talk, dance, sing, vogue, jump rope, and sit our young and old asses on the Rocks telling sweet lies, and truth or daring our way 'til it was time for the next event. Oftentimes, The Rocks was the main and only event. We were Black gay youth from the South Side who gathered our allowances to be transported to an exciting world where we were loved and celebrated for being ourselves. It was our safe space 'til it wasn't. Sometimes we were harassed by the police. We often didn't have money for clubs and were too young for the bars. I still remember a time when Black elders used to tell us they needed three pieces of ID to get in many of the clubs/bars in what was once affectionately referred to as 'Boystown.' We had school and curfews, even if we didn't always obey the rules.

"The Rocks was where we found another form of community that was accessible to me and my kind. My queer activism and self-love were developed at this magical oasis.

"I met my girlfriend/s there for dates. I kissed them there. We broke up there. The Rocks was where we drank cheap liquor, smoked, and dreamed about a better life before getting on the trains and buses to face the realities of a less dreamy, sexier existence. The Rocks was where I escaped...where we escaped to be free for a certain time by the magic and freedom of the water that reflected our special, beautiful selves inside the rainbow."

The first time Tom Segal went to the Rocks was in 1984. He had relocated to Chicago from Madison and moved into a place on Fullerton with his then-boyfriend, Brian. Both young men worked as servers at night, which meant their days were free to go to the beach. "It's funny, we started going to Fullerton Beach and then just gravitated north until eventually we were going to the Belmont Rocks," said Segal. "We were only together for a few more months, but all of a sudden, the Belmont Rocks was a part of the fabric of my life. I went there all the time."

Segal explained that he often went to the Rocks with a friend or two and that his friends preferred to lie on the rocks themselves and not the grass. "We would just lie there and cruise boys. Mostly, we would bake in the sun. In those days, it was all about the tan."

Segal recalled the summery smell in the air, "coconut oil and lotions, that beach fragrance—a good scent.

"I was fascinated by the artwork at the Rocks and how it just sort of appeared. I never saw anyone drawing or doing it—the new art was just suddenly there. The art on the Rocks was so loose and graphic and personal that I remember all of it was in contrast to the No Diving warning that was repeated on random rocks and was clearly done by the city."

Segal shared another memory of his time there. "There was a guy who bartended at Take One [2570 N. Clark]. Whenever I saw him at the bar, I thought he was so cute. One day, I was at the Rocks, and he came there with some friends. They put their towels down right beside me. I was so shy. I'm sure I was just lying there with my eyes closed, going—oh my god, oh my god, oh my god. He must have been the one who started the conversation. I know it couldn't have been me. Anyway, we started chatting and then at the end of the day we ended up going home together. It was just so perfect.

"Although the Rocks were in the middle of the city, it had a feeling of privacy. It was a place insulated from the outside world, and yet it was outside. For me, it was a place to just feel free and to be a gay boy. That place was a big part of my 20s and 30s and exploring who I was."

Segal stopped going to the Rocks in the mid-1990s. "There was a lot going on. We were all seeing a lot of death. Going there, you would see very skinny men or men with lesions, and you knew what was going on. The feeling there had changed, but mostly it was because there were so many other things happening that I stopped going."

The crowd at the Rocks for the 4th of July, 1980s. Photo by Mike Brotebeck.

Todd Brittain believes he first went to the Belmont Rocks in 1984. "I came to visit a couple of gay friends from Nebraska who had moved here. They lived on Barry [Avenue] in Lakeview. They took me to the Rocks. We were broke, and it was free, and from where they lived in Lakeview, it was right across the street."

As a visitor from Nebraska, Brittain admits the Belmont Rocks were a lot. "I was newly out to myself and to a few close friends, so I was overwhelmed. I remember that first time at the Rocks, there was a guy throwing a Frisbee in a jockstrap. Another guy sunbathing in tighty-whities. I found myself simultaneously scandalized and turned on. And the guy in the tighty-whities was doing that thing where he was sliding his sunglasses down his nose to flirt. And I was there for every bit of it. But my friends just said, 'No.'"

Brittain visited a couple more times before eventually moving to Chicago in 1991. "I remember once I took the train home from work to the Belmont stop, and I was walking east. I was about where Ann Sather is on Belmont when I noticed this guy going the other way. We cruised each other. We rubbernecked on the sidewalk and ended up walking down to the Rocks. We sat there for a while and made out and just watched the sunset."

The Belmont Rocks were a place of freedom, a place to be ourselves. 1985 photo courtesy of Norbert Shimkus.

Philip Vidal grew up on Melrose, one block north of Belmont, between Broadway and Halsted. "I attended Our Lady of Mount Carmel Grammar School on Belmont. My parents were conservative Catholics. I kept my sexuality hidden from everyone."

Vidal eventually came out in 1985 at age 26. "I mustered the courage to call Horizons on Sheffield, just north of Belmont [3225 N. Sheffield], and joined one of their coming-out groups. It was one of the best things I've ever done. I developed a strong support network through the group and certainly a better sense of myself. Later, I volunteered at Horizons and led coming-out groups.

"During the summer of 1985, some of us from the group would get together and sunbathe at the Belmont Rocks, which I remembered from its days as a Nike missile base. The guys in my group were from other parts of the city or suburbs, so the chances of them running into neighbors, straight friends, etc., was probably nil." Vidal added, "But I felt particularly emboldened when I went there since this was my neighborhood."

"Weekends and holidays, the grounds and rocks were packed with Speedo-clad guys. Attendance was about the same as Hollywood/Osterman beach is today," wrote Stanley Zimmerman in 2017. "Volleyball nets set up. Groups of friends gathered everywhere. The Rocks, in a sense, were more pleasant, no sand, no lifeguards, essentially total freedom. Many inscriptions were painted on the rocks, which made for fun reading while cruising, etc.

"In our group, there were two guys who planted flowers almost daily, resulting in a nice garden," said Zimmerman. "We would take turns dipping a bucket in the lake to water the garden. In one instance, a Chicago Park District Officer caught someone trying to pick the flowers and chased the person away, threatening arrest for defacing park property. She related the story to us the next day. We were all glad she watched over 'our' flowers."

In 1985, *Gay Chicago* columnist Rick Karlin wrote *Death on the Rocks*, a serialized murder mystery that appeared "exclusively" in the pages of the gay bar and entertainment weekly. The first chapter of *Death on the Rocks* debuted in the June 6, 1985, issue of *Gay Chicago*. On the cover that week was a pencil drawing of a Speedo-clad corpse draped across a tier of stones at the Rocks.

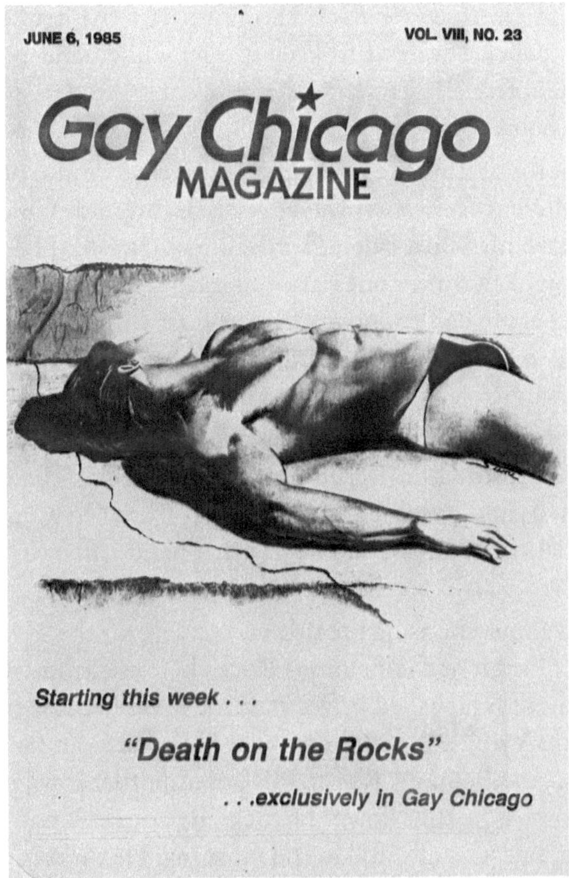

The cover of Gay Chicago *magazine issue that debuted the serialized gay whodunit* Death on the Rocks *by Rick Karlin. The installments were published weekly for the full summer of 1985 from Memorial Day to Labor Day.*

Karlin's immersive mystery series ran in weekly installments for the duration of the summer—issue after issue, a dozen entries in all, culminating on Labor Day.

When quizzed about *Death on the Rocks*, Karlin stated that the entire idea came to him in a dream. "When I woke up, I had the entire story in my head." Karlin had previously done a serialized story, *Tales of the Second City* in *Gay Chicago*. "That was mostly an homage to Armistead Maupin's *Tales of the City*, only set in Chicago." The *Tales* installments had been popular, and *Gay Chicago* wanted more.

"I wrote all of *Death on the Rocks* except the last chapter before it started printing in the paper. I wanted to keep it open-ended and turn the murder mystery into a contest. That's what we did. We marketed it so readers would write the final chapter of *Death on the Rocks*, and we would choose the winner.

"A cool twist for writing the final chapter was that we also posted clues at a number of different *Gay Chicago* advertisers around Chicago over the summer. So, there may be a clue at Little Jims [3501 N. Halsted] that says, 'Bertha Vanation has a rhinestone tiara under her bed,' things like that. So, the winning final chapter had to incorporate at least three of those clues in the chapter, and any more clues than that could be red herrings. When the panel chose the final winner, it was not my first choice."

Giving out the cash prize for penning the final chapter of *Death on the Rocks* was played to the hilt. Karlin explained, "We had the event at Bucks [3439 N. Halsted] and Ralph Paul [Gernhardt] from *Gay Chicago* came with a thousand dollars in a suitcase and he had that handcuffed to his wrist. It was very dramatic."

When asked about choosing the title and setting for the serialized mystery, Karlin replied, "I set it at the Belmont Rocks because it was where everyone went in the summer, and called it *Death on the Rocks* because the first murder takes place there. A young man, Christopher Holmes, is out for a morning run along the lake at the Belmont Rocks. His grandmother is watching from her high-rise window. As he runs down the rocks, he notices a man who looks like he's sunbathing, but it's only 7:00 in the morning. He turns out to be dead— and that starts the mystery."

Israel Wright first went to the Belmont Rocks around 1985. He was living in Harvey, Illinois, and would take the Illinois Central Railroad into the city. "The first time I came in, I went to a gay bar called Le Pub [1944 N. Clark], and people were talking, and I heard about this place called the Belmont Rocks. So, I started going there during the day on the weekends. I didn't have a car, so I depended on the train, and the Illinois Central didn't run 24 hours back to Harvey."

When Wright moved into the city to a place at Marine and Argyle, he went to the Rocks more often. "A variety of people went there, mostly diverse, and mostly everyone got along. It was a place for gay people to be with other gay people—it was about community. Some guys came to the Rocks to mess around, mostly they would meet each other and leave, but some did stuff there. Undercover cops tried to infiltrate the sex there. People would point out different guys as undercover, but mostly it was the guys having sex there that had that information."

Wright considers his experiences at the Belmont Rocks to be primarily social. "I remember more pot smoking going on there than drinking. The police were really cracking down for a while on open alcohol in the park. Many times, the people at the Rocks were not the fancy kids you saw in all the magazines, but everybody. That meant some people who didn't have anywhere to go. My main spot was right out on the lake by Belmont Harbor, so the north end of the Rocks by the parking lot. I met a number of people at the Rocks. Several of my friendships developed there.

"After the Pride Parade, the Rocks was a place for people to go who didn't feel welcome on Halsted. At some of those places, if you were Black, you might need to produce multiple forms of photo IDs, something to make people feel unwelcome. The party at the Rocks was better anyway. Frankie Knuckles was there playing music, and that was all just a great big dance party with food and everything."

Cooling off at the Rocks with a dip in the lake. Photo courtesy of Marty Hyams.

Some weekends it seemed like everyone was at the Belmont Rocks. Photo courtesy of David Klein.

Phil Bernal was 19 or 20 the first time he heard about the Belmont Rocks, but it took him a year to gather the courage to go there. "I remember seeing all the men in Speedos, all looking like they were having a blast, and I thought, 'I want that. I want to be that.' There were so many men on their towels and with their boom boxes. I thought I had died and gone to heaven."

Bernal continued, "The first time I had sex outside was at the Belmont Rocks. The Rocks was where I drank Boone's Farm Apple Wine for the first and last time. The Rocks was where I discovered my love of lying in the sun. When I think of the Belmont Rocks I remember the coconut smell of Hawaiian Tropic suntan oil. And the art, there were a lot of images and poetry on the stones, but I don't recall any porn on the stones. I swam at the Rocks, but it was important to know where to swim there. The Rocks really was the place where everyone went."

The limestone slabs that comprised the Belmont Rocks were covered with text and artwork. Both are depicted in this example. Photo courtesy of Bill M.

Randy Gresham moved to Chicago in 1978. By 1979, he was familiar with the Belmont Rocks. "It was wonderful—the Rocks were fabulous and made doubly fabulous by the writing on the Rocks themselves."

In the summer of 1980, Gresham founded the New Town Writers as a way to bring gay writers together and foster LGBT literature within a safe space. Average attendance at the meetings was approximately 10-12 members, though the number was often higher. The New Town Writers gave fellow gay writers in the group direction, advice, and encouragement.

In 1982, the group was part of the 3rd Annual Gay and Lesbian Arts Festival, a Chicago cultural showcase. As a way to promote the group and their work, the New Town Writers created the first of their yearly anthologies. The collection of poetry and prose by members was called *Off the Rocks*, and it was the first of what was to become the group's annual publication.

Gresham explained the name choice. "The Belmont Rocks was a place to hang out, relax, meet people, and have fun. *Off the Rocks* meant you can lounge around at the Rocks and relax and enjoy yourself, or you could be off the Rocks and busy working on your next masterpiece."

The second reason Gresham gave was the writing on the Rocks themselves. "There were poems and writings on the Rocks, so off the Rocks also meant taking the writing off the rocks and putting them in a collection.

"The Rocks also fostered creativity," said Gresham, recalling a surprise drag show at the Rocks. "It was in the afternoon, and it must have been a weekend. It was not a full-on drag show, but there were a few queens who performed, and the group had dancers, hunky go-go boys in Speedos, and the boys had words and phrases painted on them.

"I have very fond memories of the Rocks," added Gresham. "It was a place to have fun, share stories, swoon, and be with our own kind. And the Rocks also gave me a literary purpose as my source of inspiration."

Dogs were welcome and frequent visitors to the Belmont Rocks as seen in this late 1980s photo by Jamie Brewer.

"I had a gay brother who convinced me to move here," said Pat Cummings. In April of 1982, Cummings relocated to Chicago from Mobile, Alabama. "When I first moved here, I lived on the South Side and worked nights up here on the

North Side, so after work I went to the Belmont Rocks with a towel, and then I would take the train back home in the morning when it was safer."

After moving north, Cummings went to the Rocks more often. "Most times when I went to the Rocks at the start, I went with my brother. My brother was very scandalous, and he would hang out on the south end of the Rocks. Then I noticed some lesbians practicing softball on the grass at the north end of the Rocks and found the lesbian area up there, but because of my brother, I sort of floated between the two areas."

Cummings recalled what a great place the Belmont Rocks was to go walking with her dog, Teddy Bear...and going to the Rocks with a friend for the Air and Water Show—both of us high as kites. There was always smoke in the air at the Rocks. That's a great memory. And after I stopped drinking, I went down there and celebrated with the New Town Alano Club [909 W. Belmont]. They would have picnics down there that didn't involve alcohol. I remember they had one on Pride every year—that was a hard day for a lot of sober people.

"The Rocks had a fun energy, a cruisy energy, and there was always music going. The Rocks themselves were always painted. People used them as canvases. I miss the creativity that was going on down there. I miss the energy of the Rocks."

In 2017, Gary Lawler wrote, "There was a contingent of people through the 1970s and as late as 1986, when I left Chicago and lost historical continuity, which used the Belmont Rocks as a significant component and extension of their recovery program.

"...I think this was an important sub-group worth noting because it wasn't just about the normal Rocks' stuff. These were people who could no longer safely use the bars for socializing and community connections; [People] who were very intentionally trying to change the trajectory of their lives, and in some instances save their lives or at least prolong them. By normal Rocks standards, their interactions were probably pretty tame. But the distinctive, alcohol and drug-free location, the supporting community's approbation, and the common wellness focus offered ample opportunities to establish new, healthier friendships, social contacts, and if desired, future assignations."

In closing, Lawler added, "There are many of us alive today, and of course, many who are not, who have lived useful and productive drug-free lives because of the support, love, and understanding we received from these informal Belmont Rocks AA gatherings years ago."

Seven years after writing the above, Lawler spoke further about his life at the Belmont Rocks. "I came out of the service post-Vietnam, which was not a great time for vets," said Lawler. "I went off the deep end, but at some point, I discovered the New Town Alano Club and the other gay sober groups in the area. Part of getting sober for me was finding out who I was, who I wanted to become, and how I wanted to be gay."

The Belmont Rocks were a part of that new chapter of Lawler's life. He went there for the first time in 1981, after getting sober. "I never went there when I was drinking. When I stopped drinking, I stopped isolating and started resocializing and making friends. The Rocks was part of my new life and a place to be reabsorbed into the community. We had picnics there. It was a social spot, a gathering spot that was free. We would bring lunches and soft drinks, and water, and hang out there. The place was safe and friendly. There was sun and fresh air. There was fellowship going on there whenever you went. We would go there and 'yuk' it up, sunbathe, swim, and chat with friends. Those memories at the Rocks are deeply ingrained in my recovery and my return to the world. It was a place of meaningful friendships and important connections.

"One time a TV station sent a reporter out on assignment with a cameraman," recalled Lawler. "The reporter was walking up and down the lakefront looking for something of social interest. When she came to the Belmont Rocks, the reporter came over to our group and asked, 'Is some event going on over here? What's going on?' She asked my friend David, and he said, 'There's nothing of interest over here but a bunch of faggots.'"

Lawler also shared a Belmont Rocks memory from New Year's Day, 1987. "A friend, one of my most dedicated Belmont Rocks buddies, and I decided to inaugurate the New Year by trudging through the snow to the statue out by the Rocks. Being sober, when we got there, we each toasted the New Year with a can of Coke."

A water balloon toss at the Belmont Rocks as part of a 4th of July picnic. Photo courtesy of Robert Kimmons.

❖ ❖ ❖

Robert Kimmons came out of the closet on July 1, 1983, and went to the Belmont Rocks for the first time the same weekend. "That weekend I also went to the New Town Alano Club [NTAC] for the first time, so my first time at the Belmont Rocks was NTAC's big 4th of July picnic."

Kimmons was sober when he first went to the Rocks, but went out on a relapse later. "The next spring, maybe March or April, I was sitting out at the Rocks and was smoking some weed, and someone from the program came along walking their dog. We talked a little bit, and they said, 'Well, you could always come back.' That's what I did. So, except for that time, the Rocks was a place I associated with my sobriety. I would even meet my sponsor down there."

Kimmons attended several cookouts and parties at the Belmont Rocks hosted by the New Town Alano Club. "We would play volleyball, and we had badminton. One year, we tried to play softball. I liked going with that group because so many women in the program would be there, and most times, not a lot of women seemed to be at the Rocks, but there were a lot of women at New Town Alano Club. Those days, I felt our community was very unified, even if it was just the recovery community, but what I saw there made me know that it was a community I wanted to be a part of."

Sometimes Kimmons went to the Belmont Rocks with his friend, Nancy Reiff. "We were gym buddies, and then after we would go hang out at the Rocks. Nancy loved to lie out in the sun. If I knew the time of day, I could almost predict some of the people who would be out there, and most times I was right. Some folks would be there all day. Others would be there for two hours.

"The Rocks was a place to be social and sober. I wasn't afraid of going to bars, I was just never relaxed in them. They weren't comfortable because going to the bars seemed like it was always about sex and drinking and your looks, and your clothes. The only time I was comfortable at a bar or a club was if I just went to dance.

"At the Rocks, lots of the guys were in swimsuits, so if you were looking for someone, you knew or had a good idea as to what you were getting ahead of time. The Rocks had a 'let's have fun' approach to being social and hanging out. It felt safe to be there, because there were always more of us."

Kimmons adds, "And I especially liked it because I hate beach sand."

"When I went to the Rocks, it was a time of AIDS and everything, going there and spending time there was a way for me to decompress and let my guard down. I kept going there until probably 1993 or 1994. When I stopped going, it was due to personal and emotional issues. When all the people I used to go there to see were dead, I stopped going."

Top and bottom: Leisure gatherings at the Rocks in 1990. Cookouts, parties, picnics, the Belmont Rocks provided a perfect (and free) venue for all of the photos This page and next. Photos courtesy of Neil, 1990.

More cookouts, parties, picnics, at the Belmont Rocks. Photo courtesy of Neil, 1990.

As a Black gay boy on the South Side, I heard about this beach where it was okay to be a sissy and you would not be bothered or get beaten up," said Borris P. "So, my best friend in high school and I went to the Belmont Rocks. For our swimsuits, we cut and hemmed our gym shorts for school—they were tie-dyed and cut shorter than necessary, and we were so excited to just be there. The people were nice. It was predominantly white, but there were other Men of Color. We didn't have a blanket or anything, so people would let us camp with them for the day and use their blanket.

"Every Sunday after that, you would find us at the Belmont Rocks, sometimes even during the week. We would go to the after-hours clubs, the Warehouse [206 S. Jefferson], the Underground [Lower Links Hall, 3433-3439 N. Sheffield], The Power Plant [1015 N. Halsted], Medusas [3257 N. Sheffield]. Those places did not serve alcohol, so you didn't need an ID, and they didn't close until morning. After that, we would go over to the Rocks. Some wanted to wait until it was safer to travel back home."

"A lot of us were homeless," added Borris. "The Rocks was a safe place for gay kids to sleep all day. There were always people to watch over you. There were about five or six kids in our crew, and there were five or so other crews that hung out together for safety. We would share food with other crews if we had extra. We also would pay it forward, so if you had a good week, you might bring some sandwiches or a pack of cigarettes to share. It was a community of young people. Street kids. Every weekend was an adventure."

Borris recalled one very specific memory from 1986. "I was there during the week and saw someone I thought I knew from a distance. Dave was a

Friends at the Belmont Rocks during the 1980s. Photo by David Klein.

beautiful man, kind, with a great smile, and built like an Adonis. No one had heard from him in a while. As I got closer, I thought the man was too thin to be Dave, but then I realized that it was him. I asked if I could sit down, and he said yes. He said he had been in the hospital for a month. So, I tried to be positive and said, 'You're out now and you're going to get better.' He took his glasses off, looked into my eyes, and said, 'No, I won't. I'm dying. When I go back in the hospital, I won't come out again.' And that was what happened. But that day, we just sat, and he took my hand, and we talked. I was grateful that I was able to say goodbye to my friend. Then he thanked me and said it was great to see a beautiful face in the sunshine.

"Sometimes during the week, you would see people who were sick out there. I think they came to the Rocks to make peace, to see a kind face, or return to a place they loved. Maybe they wanted to go somewhere they felt safe at a time when people with AIDS were not welcome anywhere."

David D. would take a rock that was lower, closer to the water. "I'd tease, and guys would jump down the rocks to me. The exhibitionist in me would show them some, but my attitude was look but don't touch—very safe stuff. It was still the late 1980s. The Rocks were a great meeting place, but I wasn't looking for a boyfriend. Instead, I got off on all the sexual energy that was there. We were all just figuring out how to get our needs met at a strange time."

In the mid-1980s, Mike Donner played softball on the Touché team. "We had our practices and games on the grass there. Sometimes we would practice after work, and sometimes on Saturdays, and then our games would be on Sundays. I remember the cars driving by on Lake Shore Drive and sometimes guys yelling 'Faggots!' out the window. When they did, we would make a kind of game of it—we would all raise our arms and yell back like we were coming after them, but they were going by on Lake Shore Drive, so they weren't going to stop."

Donner also recalls the Rocks as being "very gay, but there were also a lot of other people there too. No one seemed to care. I don't recall any hassles at the Rocks themselves, just from the passing cars. After the games, a lot of bars weren't open that early, so both teams would go have drinks at the Closet [3325 N. Broadway] since it was right there and they opened early.

"Sometimes I went there with my friend Mary Beth. We would go and tan for a couple of hours before we went home and took a nap, and went out that

For years, the Belmont Rocks was the site of the gay sports leagues, including volleyball and softball. Here is Mike Dempsey playing for the Touché team when the bar was still located at 2825 N. Lincoln. Photo from the author's collection.

night. Paradise [2824 N. Broadway] was the big gay dance club we would hit at the time. That was before everything came crashing down. Probably three-quarters of the guys I played with on that softball team were lost to AIDS."

"I moved to Chicago from Lansing, Michigan," said Brian D. Smith. "But before I moved here, I used to come and visit Chicago, this was in 1983 and 1984. I would sometimes stay at my friend's place. He lived on Wellington near the lake. He worked a day job, so I would be on my own a lot of the time. I have always been drawn to water. Big bodies of water recharge me, so the Rocks were my happy place. I didn't need a beach.

"After I moved to Chicago, I went there quite a bit. For a couple of seasons, I played volleyball with the Lincoln Park Lagooners, and afterwards, there was always a barbecue or cookout at someone's place, often it was 'Ma' Bob Gammie who hosted. I met a lot of people in Chicago through the Lincoln Park Lagooners.

"It was easy to meet people anyway at the Rocks. We all used to go there. Sometimes we would have a potluck lunch there. We would sit there and dish the dirt, and people were moving around. It was a big place to hang out and a place of social connection. It was our form of social media in the day.

"The artwork on the Rocks was so colorful. There was some political stuff. Some of the art was pretty beaten up by the elements. After HIV and ACT UP, there was a lot of 'Silence=Death' and 'ACT UP fight AIDS,' sort of thing."

Smith also shared an adventure he had at the Lincoln Park Gun Club. "Once, after the gun club closed for good, but before they tore it down, we ignored the No Trespassing posts and went through a hole in the fence to look around. By then, a few people had snuck over there because the front door to the place was ajar. Inside the gun club was a trip. It was this very old-boys club and had all this masculine energy with all wood paneling. We just explored in there. I remember going into the men's room there, and it had these huge and deep six-foot marble urinals. So big you could stand in them. It's hard to forget those."

Smith added, "The best part of the Rocks was the sense of community. "Everyone seemed to go there, and it was just cool to be a part of all that. Also in those days," Smith added, "it was the style to be tan, tan, tan!"

"I heard about the Belmont Rocks before I moved here in 1985," said Bernard Garbo. "I was down in Champaign, and my friend Greg used to come up to Chicago and go to the baths and bars and then the Rocks. One time, he went out and had a little too much to drink and passed out at the Rocks and came to with some guy pulling down his pants. After that, he vowed never to go there in that condition again. That was what I had heard about the Rocks before I went there myself."

Garbo moved to Chicago in 1985, settling into a place at 1254 Lake Shore Drive. "I used to bike ride along the lakefront. That was how I discovered the Belmont Rocks for myself. I used to stop there on my ride. I would lean my bike against the top tier of Rocks and just sit a while, have a snack, and people watch. The Rocks was such a freeing space where people could be themselves, and people were themselves in so many different ways. Some sunbathed nude.

Some camped it up and were outrageous. It was a fun place to be who you wanted to be during the day and outside. Groups went there. There were lots of picnics. As I recall, there were all kinds of body types. Many people came alone or in groups and joined other people or other groups. But at the Rocks, people also left you alone if you wanted to be left alone. There was not the tension at the Rocks that there was at the bars. It was comfortable there."

"At the Rocks, I recall that people were more intimate than sexual," added Garbo. "There was some of the sex stuff, mostly at night, but sometimes during the day. More than sexual, I remember seeing a lot of intimate contact—a hand on a shoulder, a hug, kissing, holding hands. The Rocks was a safe space for people to do that kind of thing. It was important for them to be able to do that, and it was important for me to see."

My Memories of the Belmont Rocks
By Richard Knight, Jr.

"The Belmont Rocks, *the* summer gathering place for gay men back in the 1980s and 1990s, was not the haven for me that it was for hundreds of others. And I suspect; I *know* that I wasn't alone. The surface camaraderie that was to be found by being with My Tribe was trumped by my physical insecurities—as I'm sure it was for others.

"Every weekend throughout the summer, up and down Halsted Street or at the other popular hangouts for gay men back then—Carol's on Wells, Paradise on Broadway, Berlin on Belmont, Limelight in River North on Sunday nights— seemingly every conversation featured some mention of the Rocks. These two picked up each other there just last week and had found True Love; that guy was telling the bartender how he'd tricked with a hot man in the porta-potty; this gaggle of queens were all gossiping about the two hunks who 69'd under the beach towel, oblivious to the stares of all and sundry.

"I didn't need to go to the Rocks to know what I would find there. The men who found themselves in favor at the gay beach fit the rigid physical proportions of the era: the six-pack abs, bulging biceps, bubble butts, sculpted and gelled hair, impeccable tans finished off at the tanning salons on days when the sun wasn't cooperating. All as hairless as eels. The rigid physical constraints of the gay community did not have a place for anyone overweight or underweight (like moi). Scottie, one of my best friends at the time, called these perfect guys "nipple ponies," and that's how I always think of those amazing specimens of Gay Manhood as they strutted by in the bars, deigning to Bless Us with a condescending nod or on even rarer occasions, flash a smile with their gleaming pearly whites. Those of us who didn't fit the inflexible standards were invited to watch but not touch; to observe and fawn over the parade of hotties. I strongly suspected it would be the same at the gay beach. So why bother to humiliate myself?

"My friend, the jazz singer Neil—who didn't fit the hunky gay stereotype either—lived scant blocks from the Rocks. One Saturday afternoon, after we finished a recording session, he asked me to walk him back to his place. He nonchalantly lit up a joint on the street (Neil was not exactly a shrinking violet) and said, 'We deserve a treat. We're going to the Rocks.'

"What?! No way am I going to hang out with those nipple ponies."

"But Neil was nothing if not persuasive, and before I knew it, there I was, lying next to him in my loaner swim trucks and my ACT UP T-shirt, my physical insecurities over my 6-foot-2, 140-pound super skinny frame laid out for all to see on one of Neil's threadbare towels. I was quick to note that there were men of all shapes and sizes crowding every nook and cranny and that, glory be, they were all gay! But my euphoria quickly plummeted as we took in the parade of stud muffins who cruised up and down the rocky boardwalk, posing like the Greek Gods they were, ignoring the wretched masses. In other words: us. The bars were one thing, but here, these Perfect Tens had the additional benefit of being able to strut around in the nearly altogether— showing off their close to naked gym-toned bodies in their skintight Speedos instead of the usual white muscle tee and acid stone-washed jeans.

"Neil practically licked his chops, his gay porn fantasies going into overdrive. I had a few myself (I still vividly recall the Hercules in the orange swim trunks), but my fears of not fitting in, my gargantuan self-doubts, were quickly confirmed and quickly overwhelmed me. I felt awful. I finished my cigarette and excused myself, over Neil's protests, and got the hell out of there. Never to return, no matter how much Neil or other friends begged me or tried to shoo away my 'ridiculous' body issues.

"I'm not a bit regretful about not ever going back or sad that the Rocks are gone. But I am happy that what's considered physically desirable in the queer community has expanded far beyond the rigid constraints that prevailed back in the day."

Ralph and a friend at the Belmont Rocks in the late 1980s. Photo courtesy of Ralph Kennedy.

The first time Ralph Kennedy went to the Belmont Rocks was in the summer of 1985. He suspected that he first heard about the popular gay spot from his friend Victor. "When I saw the Rocks that July for the first time, I thought, oh

Kevin and Victor sunning at the Belmont Rocks in the late 1980s, from the author's collection.

my god, it's the beach nobody else wanted, but we took it over. It was ours. I hung out with friends at the Rocks and had a blast. We would always lie in the grass there, not the Rocks. Sometimes we brought inflatable floaties, though we weren't supposed to, and we would bob around in the water and listen to the music. Mostly at the Rocks you would hear dance music—a lot of the same things you heard in the bars."

Kennedy met with a core group of about ten friends at the Rocks on Saturdays and Sundays. "Saturdays were more of a maybe, but everyone showed up on Sundays. We would lie there and suntan and listen to music. We would gossip and catch up on each other's lives. Saturday was more about making plans for that night. Sundays, there was always a lot to talk about, a lot involving Saturday night. Who met someone the night before? How did everyone's evening end? We were just relaxing and checking out the crowd.

"My most memorable time at the Rocks was the day I got my nickname, so I'm reminded of it all the time. An acquaintance of ours who was a flight attendant came up to us sitting there and said to me, 'Look at you sitting there with a glass of wine and a cigarette, just like you are Rose Kennedy.' I said, 'Do not call me that.' So, of course, Rose became my nickname from that day forward."

Kennedy shared that he went to the Rocks with his best friend, Kevin V., all the time. "He died in 1992. Kevin was sick and couldn't tell people he was sick because of his work. For a while, I was his only gay friend who knew. Then he was in the hospital and couldn't keep it a secret anymore. The easiest way to tell the circle of friends was at the Rocks. So that day when we met at the Belmont Rocks, I told them about Kevin. And that day was the only day I remember crying at the Rocks."

During the mid-1980s, Tim Miller was working as a dispatcher at a trucking company in Blue Island and living in Beverly. "Friends and I used to come up from the South Side and go there and have a beer bust before heading to the bars for Happy Hour. At the Rocks, we would have fun and look at all the eye candy. We came up about once a weekend in the summer."

Sometimes, when Miller and company would come to the North Side, they would hit the bars first. "We would start out at Manhandler [1948 N. Halsted], then Sidetrack [3349 N. Halsted], which by the way, opened for business on my 21st birthday. After Sidetrack, we would hit Roscoe's [3354-56 N. Halsted], and we ended the evening at Little Jim's [3501 N. Halsted]. Once we discovered Berlin [954 W. Belmont], we went there and looked severe. After we closed Berlin, we would go to 1000 Liquors [1000 West Belmont] and get a bottle of wine and some mixers, then head to the Rocks to watch the sunrise.

"Sometimes I would go right from the Rocks to work."

In 1987, Miller relocated from the South Side to a place at 1212 West Roscoe. "That building had some parties. Five of the six units were ACT UP members. At the Rocks, I learned I was not as good a swimmer as I thought I was. In the afternoon, before one of the parties at 1212, I went to the Rocks with friends. I got in the water that day and almost drowned, but my friend, Ann, was there and wrapped her arm around my neck and pulled me to shore.

"Once we were at the Rocks," recalled Miller. "And at the time, the cops liked to zoom around on their trikes at the Rocks. One time, this cop was flying across the grass, probably trying to catch somebody doing something. He hit a ditch and went flying. We went over and checked on him, made sure he was okay, and righted his trike for him. Then he took off in the other direction, crestfallen."

Miller called the artwork on the Rocks themselves, 'amazing.' "And it was always just there. I never saw any of it being done, but it always just appeared like magic."

"Living in the neighborhood, I used to ride my bike over there during the day at least two or three times a week. The Rocks were an important part of the community outside of the bars. Even after almost drowning there, I have only fond memories of the place."

"Around 1985, when I was 20, I would go with gay friends from the southwest suburbs and lie out at the Arie Crown Forest Preserve in La Grange," said Joe Filicette, "but if we had access to a car, we drove north to the Belmont Rocks. There were usually about four or five of us."

Filicette called the endless landscape of swimsuit-clad men at the Belmont Rocks 'impressive' but added that everyone was there. "It was amazing to see all these gay people together. The Forest Preserve had some of that, but the gay people were spread out all over the park. Here, everyone was together."

In 1990, Filicette moved to the North Side and into a place at Sheridan and Irving Park. "When I moved, I went to the Rocks much more often. I used to ride my bike and meet friends there quite a bit. I got my first job out of college at Howard Brown. We used to have our staff picnics there, and all staff members would come. The Howard Brown staff was much smaller then, probably 30-40 people."

Filicette also recalled a police presence at the Rocks. "They used to drive those three-wheeled carts around. Once I was there, and a cop was in one of those things in hot pursuit of something. And the cart hit something, and the cop went flying, and the cart went off on its own. Everyone started laughing once we could see he was okay. That was memorable."

Filicette's group of friends met there regularly and always put down their blankets and towels on the grass. "We went to basically the same spot every time, which was somewhat near the strange pipe that came about three feet out of the ground in the middle of the grass.

"I love the beach, but I had never been to one with rocks before, and scary rocks too. I didn't go into the lake much when I was at the Belmont Rocks. That was why I started going to Hollywood Beach fairly early on. At Hollywood Beach, you could easily get in and out of the water."

The Belmont Rocks was also a great spot for those looking for a little afternoon delight. Photo courtesy of Paul Kubek.

In several spots, the Belmont Rocks offered "topographical camouflage." Looking down a row of slabs, there were places where single blocks buckled or toppled below the line of vision. These hidden areas were optimal for nude sunbathing and friskier goings on. If a person was engaged in behavior they didn't want visible to the general public, these recesses provided privacy—at least from most angles.

However, the greatest safety feature of the Belmont Rocks was the long stretch of lawn between the bike path and the Rocks. If the Belmont Rocks were a castle, the green was its moat. Both the police trikes and the squad cars took a bit to cross that open stretch.

Many of the guys who hung out on the top ledge of limestone were looking for sex, but they were also looking out for the police, who made sweeps of the area now and then. When the cops were present, those who noticed sent a warning to those down below. Folks might not have known one another's name, but they had each other's back. There was an unspoken pact that gay people would look out for one another.

Cruising was one of the top pastimes at the Belmont Rocks. The top row of men often kept watch to alert folks about police. 1980s photo by Gay Chicago magazine courtesy of the Legacy Project.

❖ ❖ ❖

Justin Torres first went to the Belmont Rocks in the summer of 1985. "I was with my friend Ed, and we had just left Man's Country, and we were on the way home. We ended up going to the Rocks. I was hooked from the start. When I was living across from the Vic Theater, I would go there three or four times a week. It was the place to go. There were always so many interesting people there, and a lot of the same people so you got to know them. Sometimes you would go there and start talking to someone, and then more people would come by, and then it became a barbecue with friends.

"We went there a lot at night too, after Bistro Too [5015 N. Clark] or Medusa's [3257 N. Sheffield] closed. There would be fifty people out there at night, just sitting around drinking some beers or passing around a joint or getting it on. I saw my first circle jerk there. All you really needed for a good time at the Rocks was maybe a blanket and a cooler or whatever. We went there all the time at night. I think my name was spray-painted on a couple of the rocks. The rule was never mark on a rock near the water, because in a year or so it would be underwater. The cops would come along some nights and kick us all out. Did you know the park is closed? They would kick us out, but they never did anything." Torres added, "Weather permitting, there was always something going on at the Rocks, and I always remember it being a blast. Everyone was there to have fun. It was our own little world."

In 1985, Terry Gaskins moved to Chicago from Macomb, Illinois. Shortly after relocating, Gaskins went to the Belmont Rocks for the first time. "My first job in Chicago was at a gay bar and restaurant called the Windy City Bar and Grill [3127 N. Clark]. I worked there doing mostly salad prep, but the people there told me that I had to go to the Rocks. I was underage, and there was no age limit at the Rocks, so that was the place to go.

"I had moved into a place on Fletcher around the corner from Berlin, and I had a bike. Once I went to the Rocks, I went there a lot. I went there most of the year. There were always people down there. Sometimes I would meet friends, and we would bring snacks and socialize.

"There were guys selling cans of beer for $1. If you met someone, the Rocks was a place to go chat, and that didn't cost anything.

"Mostly when I went there, I went alone and would people-watch or just sit and think about things. There was plenty of cruising going on down there, not by me, but by the guys who went there.

"I went to the Rocks less frequently as I got older, but I still went there right up until the time they were bulldozed."

A mid 1980s picnic at the Belmont Rocks with friends hanging out and enjoying one another's company. At the Rocks our bonds as a community grew stronger. Photo from the author's collection.

David Gould believes he began going to the Belmont Rocks in 1985. "I had a night job, so I would bike up and down the lakefront in the afternoons. The first time I went there, it felt like I was an outsider discovering a new land...and it was a land that was very exciting to discover. I heard about it before I went there. I can't recall where, but I thought, 'I've got to find out more about this place. I have to investigate.' So I did. The first time I went there, I didn't know anybody, but I knew that it was a welcoming place where I could feel comfortable.

"At the Rocks, people were festive and free. Swimming and cruising, and relaxing were comfortable ways to be with other gay people that was informal, not in a dark bar, and out in the sunshine. The Rocks was unique. It was a personal place and a community place and a gay beach without the beach."

Gould used to walk along the tiers of stone and admire the artwork as well. "The art there was very expressive and much of it had personal stories to it— and it was so varied. Losing that art is probably the biggest loss and regret with the Rocks being torn up and replaced."

The lawn at the Belmont Rocks provided a gathering place for larger groups, while the rocks themselves tended to attract singles and couples. Photo Marty Hyams.

Eddie Urzua was 15 in the summer of 1985—his first summer at the Belmont Rocks. "There was no kind of gay environment for queer kids. Boystown at the time was gay, male, and white. I had heard about the Belmont Rocks." Though Urzua initially had trouble locating the Rocks, when he did, he said that the sight blew his mind.

"I got to experience much of gay life there. I couldn't get into bars, so going there was eye-opening. There were so many gay men there, and I was always meeting new people. I was exposed to so many kinds of queer people, and because of that, I learned many ways to be queer. I could ask older gay adults' things. I had no access to that otherwise. The Rocks taught me how to be a young queer adult in my own way."

Urzua also noticed how race played a huge role in the gay queer community. "I didn't expect that. But as a Brown kid, it still felt like a safe space. In the day, it seemed there were all white gay kids, and at night, it was more Black and Brown gay kids. I didn't understand why there was such a division of whites from Black and Brown people, but there was, even among queer people."

Urzua also experienced first love at the Belmont Rocks. "And when he didn't return my affections, I was devastated. The whole place was such a learning experience. It held all emotions. I met so many friends there. Some of them are still friends today. I don't know how young people have those experiences now, but years ago, the Rocks was a place for it.

"Even today, when I'm driving down Lake Shore Drive, I look over to what that area is now and think, it's very nice, but the magic is gone. I'm glad I had the opportunity to go there."

❖ ❖ ❖

Hope was an especially important message as seen at the Belmont Rocks during the darkest years of the AIDS epidemic. Photo courtesy of Bill M.

Humor was another key element of the artwork at the Belmont Rocks.

Peter D. Reid was 22 when he moved to Chicago in June of 1985. He had a job lined up that started in a week. Being broke, he ended up staying at the SRO hotel, the Abbott, aka 'Chicago's Gay Hotel,' 721 W. Belmont.

"My first day in Chicago was one of those warm summer evenings. I had a bike, so I rode my bike towards the lake. And as I did, I kept seeing all these handsome men going this way, and they were checking me out too. Then, when I got to the yacht club, I veered south and saw these groups of men on the grass—so I went closer. I got to the top of the Rocks. Stretched out below me on the Rocks were 100 men...a sea of men in Speedos. I thought, 'Oh my God, I have discovered 'the place.'' I had a book with me, and I sat with my back against the wind fence and took it all in. There was shooting from the gun range to the south. Sitting there, I met a good friend of mine, Kevin, who remains a good friend today."

After that first evening, Reid went to the Rocks regularly. "I went to the Rocks as often as I could and built an amazing collection of friends. Going to the Belmont Rocks was what we did. Every weekend around 10 or 11 a.m., I

Peter Reid at the Rocks

would take my umbrella and beach gear, go to the Rocks, and stay all day. There were food vendors, water vendors, hot dog guys, and beer guys. Those days at the Belmont Rocks with that circle of 10 or 11 of us was sort of a kumbaya circle. We talked about everything. All those friends died one by one. The only two left are Kevin and I.

"The Rocks were a place to meet and make connections, and that doesn't happen anymore. It was a place to do that, which wasn't a bar, so if you didn't want to drink or weren't 21, you could go there and you could find your crew. The Rocks was free, and they also presented a broader spectrum of people. The place was there in an age of innocence, at a time when if a person was gay, that meant they were automatically trustworthy. That isn't true anymore, so there wasn't the current guardedness."

Reid believes that after 1990, the popularity of the Rocks began to wane. "They became less the place to be as Hollywood Beach began to develop. My favorite memory of the Rocks was when I rode my bike there one morning at dawn. I neglected to mention, I am a fisherman, and I was going to my regular fishing spot, but instead took off all my clothes and just sat in this hidden cove and watched the sun come up. There were only about three or four people out there for the sunrise, and we all had our space. As I was sitting there naked, all these white fish began breaking the surface. The water that morning was so clear you could see right into the lake. I fished down there in the nude for about an hour and caught probably six or seven fish. It was magical."

In 1985, photographer Doug Ischar began an interesting experiment. Every nice day that summer, he went to the Belmont Rocks and visually documented the experience. The photos he took that summer capture much of the vibrancy and energy of the Belmont Rocks. Ischar's 1985 photography experiment spawned the exhibit Marginal Waters in 2009, almost 25 years later.

Claudine Ise wrote about the *Marginal Waters* exhibit for *Artforum* magazine. "The languorous tangles of seminude men in Doug Ischar's photographs resurrect lost moments in queer urban history. Heads resting against thighs, hands reaching across bare torsos to stroke damp hair; the glazed eyes and drowsy expressions of these men result not from sex or drugs but from the pleasures of sun and heat. Taken in the summer of 1985 at a gay lakeside hangout in Chicago known as the Belmont Rocks (removed in 2003 as part of a revetment project), Ischar's images capture an era through its cultural effects: gold chains and zebra-striped bikinis, an outdated issue of *Vanity Fair* under a book about Diane Arbus, a pink plastic flamingo perched jauntily next to a dozing sunbather."

The exhibit resulted in an accompanying 68-page book called *Marginal Waters* (2009) published by Golden Gallery, Inc. Unfortunately, the book with photos from the exhibit is currently out of print, and secondhand copies have become quite costly.

Doug Ischar's Story

After moving here from San Francisco in 1983, Ischar settled into a place at Broadway and Cornelia. "I was new in town. I wanted to know where to cruise and where the gay bars were. I went from there. The first time I went to the Rocks, I was amazed that this gay beach was in the middle of town. Even in San Francisco, the gay beach was removed and remote, but the Belmont Rocks were right in the middle of things. Very obvious and very unapologetic."

Ischar enrolled in a photography class at Columbia College, though he'd hardly picked up a camera before. "Looking around for subject matter, it suddenly hit me like lightning that this was what I had to be doing. I had left San Francisco, where the AIDS crisis was more extreme. Chicago was behind in terms of the spread and awareness of the disease. I wanted to record something I cherished. At the Rocks, I was struck by the historical value of the place, and so I sort of became a conservationist with a camera. That was my passion for the project.

"I have had people say that since the photos in *Marginal Waters* were taken in 1985, why don't they focus more on AIDS. But the Belmont Rocks pictures were taken for that reason. Things were looking grim in 1985. We weren't sure if AIDS was

The author with noted Belmont Rocks and "Marginal Waters" photographer Doug Ischar prior to a 2018 WBEZ interview about the importance and legacy of the area. Photo from the author's collection.

going to wipe us all off the face of the planet or if we all might be forced back in the closet or what. So these pictures, showing gay men enjoying one another in a spontaneous and unconstructed way, were a preservation effort, and that's why I called myself a conservationist with a camera."

Striving to capture the Rocks scene as it was, Ischar shunned posing by his subjects. "Ideally, they would not even know I was there. I wanted to photograph these men living, going on with their lives, and at ease with one another. I wanted to be a fly on the wall. I almost never asked permission. If I had, I would have gotten a different kind of picture—posed, smiling, looking into the camera. The last thing I wanted was to elicit people's attention and disturb things...recording this remarkable place and the beauty of the subculture that lived here was well worth any potential embarrassment. Gay white men have done a very good job of insulating themselves from documentation because they often have the class clout, the money, and the privilege to be protected from photographers interested in the social experiment they are involved or engaged in.

"The most magnificent thing I ever saw at the Rocks involved the cops," said Ischar. "There were some cops who would kind of threaten the place by driving through the park in their cruisers—very threatening and intrusive. One day, I saw a whole slew of gay men line up and give this intrusion the Nazi salute. For some reason, I didn't photograph that. Maybe I was just standing back in awe."

Ischar has a favorite photo from his *Marginal Waters* collection. "There was one picture I took of a sort of working-class, marginal guy in terms of class identity. Anyway, I got a shot of this guy slipping off his wedding ring. That is one of my favorite pictures, one of those shots that was just astonishing luck."

For Ischar, the secret to getting the perfect photo is to "Shoot a lot of film. I learned early on that my batting average was not great. To get the pictures I wanted, I had to take a lot of shots. The beauty of 35mm photography is that you can shoot a lot and edit later. I would shoot with abandon and hope I got something.

I got some of the most remarkable shots in that series by staying put and shooting the same scene with the elements in the picture changing in subtle ways. I would do that until things fell into place, that is why some of the pictures seem set up. I never set anything up."

The first year that Ischar shot the world of the Belmont Rocks was 1984. However, that year he took the photos with black and white film. "Those photos are more concerned with a sort of body sculpture, and although that was aesthetically beautiful, it ultimately was not what I wanted. What I wanted to capture was really an in-depth portrait of the subculture. For that, I needed color." Ischar began shooting with color film the following summer.

"That was also a time in photography when image-text art, photographs with text, was kind of the rage," added Ischar. "So, I thought I would do my own sort of image-text work by finding the text in the environment. So the Rocks photos are actually quite full of book covers, magazine covers, those kinds of things, which say a lot about the people reading them. There's a picture of a young man who fell asleep with his pink flamingo stuck in the grass beside him. People brought the most astonishing things with them, and I wanted that color—literally and metaphorically—to be present in the work. That's why I switched to color pictures.

"The Rocks were a liberating environment," said Ischar, "a good example of a radical environment. I felt the Rocks, especially for the Midwest, had the importance and charge of a radical experiment."

Dan Bell had his most memorable summer at the Belmont Rocks in 1986, a time he refers to as the Season of the Cave.

"When I was shown the cave, I quickly became one of the unofficial tour guides. You entered and exited from the water. It wasn't safe to do on a rough sea day. The lighting in the cave was really interesting. You had the blue-green glow from the water entrance on the east and then some sunlight coming down from a small opening at the back or west side of the cave. It had a hard, dirt bottom. You could comfortably get about six people in there. One time, as I was leading a couple of guys in there, when I popped out of the water, there were two guys completely naked having sex. It was the perfect spot for that. I only experienced it for a season. A winter storm created the cave, and a winter storm destroyed it.

"Many people found it too spooky to go into the cave. You had to swim underwater through a tunnel and then come up on the other side. You could only access the cave when the lake was calm. It was probably 20 feet across and maybe five feet high—you could almost stand in there," said Bell. "The cave formed when the Rocks shifted in the winter. Who found it? I have no idea, but I went in there probably 20 times over that summer."

Bell went to the Belmont Rocks for the first time several years earlier, when he moved to Chicago in 1978. "The Rocks were amazing, a unique experience to see that many gay guys with so little on, combined with all these great views of the lake. Water is therapy for me, and the social scene at the Rocks was always interesting. I liked to go there during the week, mostly in the morning when it was quieter."

Bell's partner, Tom Gillengerten explained that the two men lived together at several addresses in the vicinity of the Rocks. "We would walk over. We had lots of friends in the high rises around there, but the Rocks were in many ways a meditative place for me."

Gillengerten continued, "I used to take a collapsible fishing rod in my backpack and go there and fish early in the morning. I could sit there for hours. Fishing was meditative. I caught mostly perch there, but also rainbow trout, as well as smallmouth bass. I remember people flying kites at the Rocks on the grass and how sometimes in the summer there were days when the dragonflies seemed to be everywhere."

The two men also recalled the artwork at the Rocks, which Bell described as "interesting words and affirming statements. The creativity of what was put down on the Rocks was special and added to the uniqueness of the space."

Gillengerten was an admirer of the artwork and a contributor as well. "I knew people who had carved and painted things on the Rocks. At the time, I was infatuated with pigeons, so I painted a pigeon on the Rocks. I liked adding something to the artwork there and becoming a part of that community as well."

Sunning on the lawn at the Rocks. Photo courtesy of Mike Brotebeck.

The first time Mike Jefvert went to the Belmont Rocks was in the summer of 1986, shortly after moving into the neighborhood. "I think I heard about the Rocks at the gay video bar Take One [2570 N. Clark]. Not long after that, I walked down to the lake looking for the Rocks and not knowing quite where it was, and then all of a sudden it was—Oh, here it is."

The Belmont Rocks was where Jefvert discovered and socialized with his circle of friends. "There was a core group of about eight or nine of us, and a few others who would come and go. After a while, we didn't even make plans to meet. We would just assume some people in our group would be there in our spot every Saturday and Sunday. We put our blankets down near that pipe that came out of the ground. We called that area our 'time share.' When I think of that lawn at the Rocks, all I can see are blankets and bicycles, because there weren't bike racks down there.

"We usually got there in the late morning to 'work on our tans,' and we usually stayed until after 4 p.m. We would stay there all day and just take in the sun, check out the guys, talk, share silly stories, and just bond. We talked about health, too. We became tremendous friends. None of us had boyfriends. We

112

The gays bringing posh spa glamour to the Belmont Rocks. Photos courtesy of Mike Brotebeck.

all said we wanted one, but I don't think we did really. And we were one group. There were groups like ours all up and down the beach. On Saturdays we would go home, shower, and then go back out. On Sundays we were more likely to leave the Rocks and go right to Sidetrack [3349 N. Halsted] or to Big Chicks [5024 N. Sheridan] for the Sunday cookout."

Jefvert refers to the Rocks as part of his coming-out experience. "It was a way of submerging myself into gay life after a long time of trying to push gay life away. The Rocks was a place to be yourself and discover who you were. Coming out and dealing with that meant dealing with the reality of HIV. We were able to share all the fears that came with having this disease lurking among us.

"My favorite Rocks memory was one crazy hot Fourth of July. We were at the Rocks as usual, and my friend Bob showed up wearing a white terrycloth robe with a matching towel wrapped around his head in a turban. He had a cigarette in one hand and was wearing this ridiculous rhinestone ring that was as big as a silver dollar. It is just a random memory, but I still laugh thinking about that."

Jonathan "Yoni" Pizer moved to Chicago from Madison, Wisconsin, in the autumn of 1986, settling in Hyde Park near the campus. Soon after relocating, Pizer met Brad [Lippitz], a third-year law student at the University of Chicago. Their first date was on November 23 of that year. Pizer realized quite soon that he had met the man he would be with for the rest of his life.

The following spring, Brad and Yoni got their first place together. "We were in Edgewater, and Brad was the one who took me to the Belmont Rocks. He had told me about it, and I really didn't understand, but getting off my bike and looking around, I thought, 'This is amazing.' I liked the laid-back nature of it. There were no signs, no advertising, the Rocks were just something people knew about as a place to be yourself in the middle of the city."

Brad Lippitz had a tough time recalling when he first went to the Rocks. "I went to undergrad school in Champagne, and I think it was one year when I was home for the summer. I remember when I saw it, thinking it was like the *Wizard of Oz*. I mean, you just turned a corner, and you were dancing around the maypole. There were guys running around, some guys in the water, people were having picnics—everyone was playing and sunning and swimming and

The late 1980s, love at the Rocks. Brad Lippitz and Yoni Pizer were fond of Frisbee, hacky sack, and socializing at the Belmont Rocks. Photo courtesy of Brad Lippitz.

being together. This was an area with people being open and free; there was nothing clandestine about it at all. After Yoni and I moved north, we went there all the time. The Rocks was free, accessible, and not too far away—it was public and yet, it offered some privacy."

"We mostly rode our bikes and went by ourselves," said Pizer, "but the Rocks was a great place to meet people. It was so social there, but it's easy to be social in a Speedo. We also brought a Frisbee, which is a great way to meet people."

Lippitz recalled hacky sack as being another pastime they enjoyed at the Rocks. "But you didn't need to do anything, it was just so nice there; pleasant and relaxing, though the swimming was treacherous. The artwork and graffiti there was playful and political, and reflective of the community. It was a joyful place. Once a friend of ours was having a birthday, and we asked him what he wanted, and he said, 'Oh, just maybe something at the Rocks.' So we got some food together, music, and beer, and had his party at the Rocks—and it was terrific, and the ideal setting.

"When we got there, we usually stayed on the grass and just tipped our bikes beside our towels," recalled Pizer. "I have only fond memories of going there. People were always coming and going, and they were mostly fun people. The Rocks wasn't a bar. It was open and beautiful with the lake and the views of the city skyline, especially to the south."

Pizer continued, "Brad and I went there right up until the end. We made a point to do so. We weren't alone. People were still going to the Rocks. There was still a consistent parade of folks going there until it was closed down by the Army Corps of Engineers, and then it wasn't a thing anymore."

"The days were joyous there," added Lippitz. "I see the allure of Hollywood Beach, but there was definitely sadness in saying goodbye to the Rocks. I lamented that loss."

At the Rocks you could be social or you could keep to yourself. There were no expectations. Photo Phillip Michael Holda.

Phillip Michael Holda moved to Chicago in 1987 with his college boyfriend after attending Michigan State University. "Our first apartment happened to be on North Sheridan Road between Wellington and Barry, facing Lake Michigan, where I had a perfect view of the Belmont Rocks. I remember the first time I went there; I was amazed at how freely the boys were with their gayness—this was all new to me. I had never seen guys holding hands, kissing, and just loving each other out in the open like this, especially in the daytime! This was a very freeing time for me. I loved going down there and lying out in the sun with the friends I met in Chicago, who I am still in contact with today. We would gawk at all the hot boys, buy beer from the guy walking around with the cooler, and enjoy the sea of gayness."

Carl Szulczynski was a bisexual teenage runaway from Kentucky when he found a safe space at the Belmont Rocks. "I'll never forget the day I joined the Horizons LGBT youth group. It was filled with the most colorful people I had ever seen. After my first group meeting, I followed some kids around. They ended up at the Rocks, and so did I. My mind was blown with every step closer to the sunbathing angels in their Speedos and jock straps, and sometimes nothing at all. The scent of coconut oil aroused my every sense as I waded through the narrow paths between sunbathing, oiled-up, muscled beauties, and boom boxes blasting Depeche Mode. I was literally a kid in a candy store."

One day, Carl arrived at the graffiti-colored rock that his group chose as their spot and saw Carlos. "His thick, black hair was slicked back off his smooth, sculpted face. His package lifted straight upwards in his tight, little Speedos. I had to have him, and I did. It was easier than I thought, even though he pretended to tease. He couldn't resist any more than I could. But neither of us was ready for a relationship. We had just discovered our new playground, and we could play well together. So we did."

Carl and Carlos made themselves at home at the Rocks from 1985-1993. "We carried our Belmont Rocks 'slutwear' look all over town in spandex, and other, over-the-top, hypersexual fashions. We kept Bad Boys [3311 N. Broadway then 3352 N. Halsted] and Flashy Trash [3524 N. Halsted] in business with our regular purchases of stripper gear," said Carl.

"The Rocks would be the setting of much of my life's drama, and the occasional, anonymous sexual encounter. It was not without its comedy, however. Such as the time I saw another beautiful, young Mexican boy. He

Carl Szulczynski at the Belmont Rocks circa 1990. Photo courtesy of Carl Szulczynski.

couldn't speak English, so I asked Carlos how to say 'Hello handsome' in Spanish. He repeated a phrase for me until I memorized it, and I nervously approached the young man and said the words. I wasn't expecting the response I got. The boy looked at me with confusion and a little bit of attitude. Apparently, Carlos had played a trick on me. Instead of saying 'Hello handsome,' I just went straight to 'I want to suck your dick'....

"Carlos was always getting me into trouble. Like the day we were chilling on the rocks, ignoring the no swimming signs and skinny-dipping offshore. He saw a yacht a few hundred yards away with a palm tree on the deck. He insisted it was his friend, so he waved at the yacht. The occupants waved back. Carlos wanted to swim all the way to the yacht, so we did. We were utterly exhausted, and it took every ounce of energy I had to swim all the way out there. Once we got there, Carlos realized that he didn't know any of these guys after all. Lucky for us, they were all sexy, horny men, and they greeted us warmly...We partied for hours until they finally escorted us back to shore on a dinghy. My little brother William would join Carlos and I, and eventually we became a trio of fierceness. And while I would move on to Miami, New York, L.A., and other amazing cities, I would never forget the Belmont Rocks or the many special times I had there. It was the best playground a boy could have ever hoped for ..."

Seven years later, in 2024, Szulczynski called the Belmont Rocks "a safe place for a young gay boy in the big city without any family. Back in 1985, I went there every chance I could get. It was an exciting place where I learned. I used to go there and lie in the sun with my eyes closed, listening to the conversations going on around me. I learned a lot just by listening to my elders talking. Most guys were nice. There were some dirty old men in thongs, which I still cannot relate to—I mean, now I'm a dirty old man myself, and I still would never wear a thong in public.

Something important to say is that I am actually bisexual. When I ran away, I was a 15-year-old Kentucky boy married to a 32-year-old woman. I think bisexual visibility is important. After I got to Chicago, it was just easier to say I was gay because people didn't believe you when you said you were bisexual. But the gay community was still more accepting of bisexuality than the straight community. Even as a bisexual, I felt I fit in at the Belmont Rocks. When I went there, I mostly accepted and embraced the gay part of my identity.

"We went to the Rocks all the time. We would hang out and usually try to cop a six-pack or a joint and just chill. I hung out there with my friends a lot from ages 16 to 18. Then I moved to Indiana for a while. When I returned to Chicago at age 21, I went right back to the Rocks. That was still the social spot, and it was still just as fun. That was when I would bring my teacup Yorkie, Chiquito, with me to the Rocks. He always attracted people. Everybody wanted to pet Chiquito. I remember one line guys used was, he's so cute, and the dog isn't bad either.

"Since those days, I have lived in cities all over the world, and the Belmont Rocks remains so unique—it was a place very specific to Chicago, to our movement and our community."

❖ ❖ ❖

"I went to the Rocks for the first time in the summer of 1987," said Paul Kubek, "and went a few times a week through 1991. There was a sense of community at the Rocks. I was in college and in a relationship, and this was a way for me to be a part of the community in a safe space. Going there widened my sense

Top and bottom, more sun and surf at the Belmont Rocks. Photos courtesy of Paul Kubek.

Photos courtesy of Paul Kubek.

of community. The Rocks were also a part of my bigger coming-out process. I was releasing internalized homophobia and learning to just let loose. Plus, there were also hot guys there in bathing suits. I had friends who went there at night to cruise, but I never did that."

Around 1988, Kubek began taking pictures at the Belmont Rocks. "It was one of the few places that I saw gay guys interacting outside of a bar. That was rare. And it wasn't as though a camera was welcome in the bars. But no one said a word at the Rocks. I didn't go there specifically to take pictures, but I brought the camera with me and took them. I photographed a lot of the graffiti as well. I wanted to document this place and gay life at the Rocks."

Stephen Sinclair lived in several major metropolitan areas before moving to Chicago in 1987 to attend music school. When he arrived in town, Sinclair settled into a place on Surf near the popular gay bar Bulldog Road [2914 N. Broadway]. "That was probably where I heard about the Rocks," said Sinclair. "There were some people there who said to me, 'You have to come and swim with us on the next full moon.' So, I did. The next full moon, we gathered at the Rocks. The night was beautiful. It was hot, but there was a nice breeze off the lake. The water was perfect, and the moon was coming up and glistening on the water. And we all just took off our clothes and slipped into the water. It was so hot outside, and the water felt great. It wasn't a sexual thing or a radical faerie thing, just a group of gay guys hanging out together. There was a group of us that swam in the lake nude during the full moon each month in the summer. Mostly, we would just float around and talk. No one harassed us. The Rocks was a safe space for our nude clandestine moonlight swims every month. I swam with that group for a couple of years. I loved nude swimming, but I started getting more involved in ACT UP. Things changed, and it seemed like I didn't really have the time anymore."

I met Jeff Fields through mutual friends, but got to know him from hanging out at the Belmont Rocks. Jeff often rode his bike there on sunny days. He would come and sit down or stretch out in the sun beside me and chat. Sometimes it was the two of us, and sometimes we were in larger groups. At first, I was nervous. Jeff was movie-star gorgeous. He was also a wonderful singer with the voice of a crooner. His looks and voice made him seem like a 1950s idol. Jeff seemed as though he belonged in a different era.

Jeff quit drinking before I met him, which was extremely unique among my friends at the time. He had been through a lot, but instead of hardening him, those difficulties made him an extremely kind and compassionate man. I remember the small red scar, or was it a birthmark, he had on one cheek. He had another puckered scar on his chest. Jeff loved to go two-stepping and vocalists like Barbara Cook, k.d. lang, and Rosemary Clooney. Jeff was funny, a great listener, and the kind of person I wanted to be.

I have a picture of Jeff at the Belmont Rocks. In the photo, he is lazing on the rock above me—his love of the sun is clear. Jeff said he enjoyed the warmth of lying on the limestone blocks. In moments like those, Jeff seemed like a cat. Present. Relaxed. Languishing.

The photo of him brings the moment back so clearly.

Jeff was one of the many lost during the AIDS epidemic. He was in his late thirties when he passed away on May 9, 1996.

The late Jeff Felds sunning at the Belmont Rocks in 1989. From the author's collection.

In his essay 'How Queer People Reinvented the Beach,' Michael Waters explored the queer claiming of several public spaces using several examples, one of them the Belmont Rocks. In the piece, Waters quotes the essay 'Imminent Domain' by Christopher Reed. "Queer placemaking involves the transformation of 'what the dominant culture has abandoned so that old and new are in explicit juxtaposition.' A queer space, to Reed is a 'space in the process of, literally, taking place, of claiming territory.'"

Reed told Waters, via email, that he penned the essay after spending the summer of 1995 at the Belmont Rocks. Reed was impressed by the 'sense of spontaneous community' at the Rocks. They seemed to embody this strand of guerrilla placemaking—a social hub fashioned out of almost nothing."

In the late 1980s and into the 1990s, John O'Brien resided at 444 W. Belmont. With the Rocks so near, O'Brien ended up frequenting the gay beach. "A few friends would meet at our place and get our floats and inner tubes, and coolers, and all the gayness we could muster, and head over to the Rocks. Sometimes we would rollerblade over. There were usually somewhere between five and ten of us. This was before cellphones, but if anyone was late, they knew where we were."

O'Brien went there primarily during the week. "Even then, there was a nice crowd. We were mostly restaurant people, bar people, teachers…When we went there, we were out to get five good hours of sun. It was a full day. There were vendors selling cold beer, popsicles, sandwiches, and joints. Some people utilized the lawn with canopies and tents for barbecues. The Rocks were a big dog place, too. Lots of people brought their dogs there. The entire thing was a patchwork of festive blankets and umbrellas and everything. People would go from camp to camp and from one group to the next, visiting. Folks were always passing joints around, and it was a place of freedom.

"The Rocks was a place to behold. Some days, we would link our floats in a circle in the water and just talk like that. If someone wanted to skinny dip or lie out naked, no one really cared. No one bothered about things there too much, at least when I was there. No outside bullying that I ever saw. It was all very peaceful."

Anything might happen at the Rocks. Photo courtesy of John O'Brien.]

❖ ❖ ❖

Susana Darwin moved to Chicago in May of 1988. Her job had ended in Boston, where she hadn't really enjoyed living. "I was eager to get back to the Midwest. I was aware of the Belmont Rocks and its reputation as a gay-friendly place, so my first weekend in Chicago, I made my way there. A group playing pick-up volleyball was wonderfully welcoming—various ages, ethnicities, and genders. The afternoon was magical: balmy weather, bright sunshine, sweet company, Lake Michigan in its usual salutary self.

Above: Volleyball at the Belmont Rocks. Photo courtesy of Neil.
Below: Playing ball at the Belmont Rocks. Photo courtesy of the late Ron Ehemann.

"The following Monday, during a chat with my mom, she observed, 'You're in a new city. You don't have a job. You're a long way from your girlfriend. But you sound happier than I've heard you sound in ages!' A treasured, anchoring memory.

"I don't know if I ever saw any of those people who were playing volleyball that day ever again, but being invited to join in their game put me in a mindset of being open to meeting people and trying new things. That day was instrumental in why I stayed in Chicago for 30 years and why I felt that it was the right place for me to be."

I Had to Step Over Two Lesbians Having Sex to Get to the Rocks
By Mary Harvey

"Let's go to the rocks.

"Traffic is stacked up on Belmont in a long, lazy stretch from the Drive to just before Sheridan Avenue. Music and voices float through the summer air. The sun has only been down for a couple of hours, but the heat feels like noon.

"The car is filled with gay kids escaping the South Side of Chicago for another Friday night that our parents will never know about. Torn Guess and 501 jeans, Converse All-Star High Tops and high-sided Reeboks, Ocean Pacific and B.U.M. Equipment T-shirts. Hair moussed to the point of brushing the car's ceiling. Earrings and makeup.

"Where?

"A couple of them haven't been there before. Necks are craning to see what I am talking about as I exit the drive at Belmont, waving vaguely over to my right at a huge, empty darkness that doesn't, at first glance, look like anything but huge empty darkness. We pull into the parking lot.

"C'mon.

"A boom box (an extremely large portable music player with a radio station and a one or two cassette player/recorders, with a carrying handle) is hauled out of the trunk.

"Where are we going?

"Apprehension. The two that haven't been there before start to lag behind. It's an awfully big darkness, with a wide swath of lawn, a few trees scattered about, and a long section of uneven rocks braced right up against a lake that is virtually always temperamental. On particularly rugged nights, you can hear the waves from the parking lot. There are no lights at all except for one aging yellow burner over the lot, its feeble light swallowed up by the night.

"Let's go.

"We move forward, the blackness swallowing us up. The two laggers start to hurry, afraid of being left behind.

"My friends and I plunge ahead. It's too early for partying, or it's after a party and too early to hit the Melrose Café just yet. We don't have enough fake IDs to get everyone into the bars. The Horizon's Youth Group closes up the meet-and-greet at 9 p.m. We don't have anywhere else to go.

"I can hear groaning in the darkness. The two newbies behind me freeze in their tracks. "What the hell is that?

"I don't see the two shapes rolling and grappling on the grass until I almost trip over them. It's two women, oblivious to the world around them as they get lost in their lovemaking. My friends and I split around them like a herd of buffalo moving around a boulder on the trail.

"In about an hour, I will be doing the same thing with my girlfriend. Yes, on the ground.

"Even with people all around, there was an odd sense of privacy. What happened on the Rocks stayed on the Rocks. Even in daylight. There was some unspoken agreement that we were all there for something, whether it was teenagers blasting their boom boxes in the middle of a hot summer night or single people cruising or partiers hanging out until it was time to get breakfast and go home.

"It was our place. The place we went to when there was nowhere else to go.

"We broke up with or found lovers there. We held impromptu dance parties, with the rocks providing the best props ever as we jumped up and twisted to the music. We clustered in groups, boys and girls, budding young queens and transpeople, Black and white, Hispanic and Latino/a, Asian and

Arab. GLBTQ teenagers didn't belong on the South Side. Or the West Side. The North Side was only for adults. We fit exactly nowhere.

"So, we went to the Rocks. Where we could drink alcohol, smoke pot, light candles and incense sticks, have sex, listen to music, sunbathe, and write in notebooks whatever was on our minds or in our hearts. We emptied out everything we'd been holding inside all week long in the places where we slept, worked, and went to school. Back home, we simply existed.

"But we lived at the Rocks.

"It was a few hours a weekend, but the world could shift on its axis in that time. A girl you loved might lean in close and whisper in your ear that yes, she was into you. Or she might show up holding hands with another girl. Or you could spend the entire time trying to talk a gay friend out of his tear-stained grief storm because his lover just dumped him.

"The best was when we'd hit the Rocks after a Saturday Horizons Youth Group meeting and hang out for hours, bonding with people we'd never met before but who all lived in the same city.

"The beaches belonged to everyone. But the Rocks belonged to us. It wasn't a place. It was a point in time. There we were not alone. It was the complete opposite of the overwhelming loneliness that dogged us week in and week out. There was love. Community. You found a powerful truth: It wasn't just you, out there on your own. There were other LGBTQ teens in the world. You realized that your story was framed within a much larger story. You understood that you shouldn't judge yourself or anyone else, because we are all struggling. And we are all in this together."

Several years after the above reminiscence, Mary Harvey spoke further on life at the Belmont Rocks. "At Horizons, there was a Friday night drop-in Youth Group meeting and a Saturday discussion group. I had just turned 18 and lived on the South Side. I went almost every Saturday, and it took almost an hour to get to Horizons. I started going there in the winter. I kept hearing people talk about the Belmont Rocks. When I asked what the Belmont Rocks were, the others said something like, 'Just the coolest place on earth.'"

Harvey learned more about the Rocks the following spring. "It wasn't even that warm out yet, but after that Saturday meeting, we got something to eat and went to the Rocks. As we were walking across the grass, I saw the Rocks from a distance. They didn't look like anything special. We have rocks like that along the lakefront on the South Side, too. But they just said, 'You'll see.' This place was Mecca to them.

"As soon as we got to the Rocks themselves, the others started scrambling all over the stones. It was the happiest I had seen these people in two or three months. We went there after every meeting because this was our place. And that was our routine. We would go to the meeting, load up on food, and then go to the Belmont Rocks. There were usually about ten boys and three girls, although there were sometimes more girls.

"The Rocks was also a good place to go after the meetings because sometimes people shared some very intense things at those meetings. It was clear that they were going through something rough. When that happened, we would circle around that kid after the meeting. We made sure they got something to eat, because it was very important to ensure they had something in their stomach. Then we would go to the Rocks and bring them along, and slowly you could see them de-escalate. Sometimes, after what they shared, seeing a place where they could be free would help a lot. We could also have a sort of group therapy part two. People could talk individually or bring up things they didn't feel comfortable bringing up in a group setting. Just breathing the air helped a lot, too. Deep breaths. Fresh air. The Lake. That was therapy. Water helps you to give it all up and let everything go.

"We could share more there. The boys in the group saw all the guys in Speedos and they were like, ok, I guess life does go on. We would bring a boom box. We did a lot of dancing on the Rocks, hours of dancing. The Rocks was our dance floor. We would even bring cardboard and break dance there. Sometimes we managed to get some beer. We were being normal teenagers. Straight kids could do this anywhere. We got to do it at the Belmont Rocks. Those days are still treasured memories," added Harvey. "I miss the Rocks with all my heart, and I am so glad we had a place to go where we could be ourselves and be accepted without hassles or harassment."

Art around the Rocks could be funny and carried messages. Photo author's collection.

Adam Azus remembers. "Saturday afternoons, going to the Rocks after our meeting at Gay Horizons Youth Group, we would go to Ricky's Restaurant, [3181 N. Broadway] for lunch, then hang out at the Rocks the rest of the afternoon. I was an awkward teenager in a cowboy hat and daisy dukes. My friends [and I] on several occasions added our own art to the Rocks."

❖ ❖ ❖

From the 2019 obituary of Ragnar "Rag" Hammerberg in the Windy City Times, a friend of the former Chicago resident said, "Ray was a gay icon during the 1980s as the premier bartender at the Gentry Bar on Rush Street [712 N. Rush]. Besides being very handsome and charming, he was quite the sun worshiper. He even had his own rock at Belmont Beach on which to sunbathe back in the day."

Another pooch at the Belmont Rocks. Photo courtesy John O'Brien.

William Sigler remembered. "In the late 1980s, my friend Michael and I were going from the yacht club to the Rocks. As we were walking along, we saw what looked like a brand-new Sony Discman lying on the bottom level of the Rocks down by the water. So, I went to get it, and when I grabbed the Discman, the headphones were attached, and it was then that we saw they were in the ears of a dead man who was in the water. This was before there were cellphones, so we ran to the pay phone outside the yacht club and called 911. The operator asked if I knew CPR, and I said no, but I know a dead man. He had been dead for a while. We figured he slipped on the Rocks, hit his head, and drowned."

❖ ❖ ❖

In 1988 photographer Billy Howard photographed the founders of TPAN at the Belmont Rocks. The photo was later published in Holward's book, Epitaphs for the Living. *Photo courtesy of Howard and TPAN.*

The Test Positive Aware Network is a grassroots HIV support organization and peer group that began operations in 1987. In 1988, Billy Howard photographed the founders of TPAN at the Belmont Rocks on a blustery day. The shot captures the members of the group looking united and strong as they brace against the wind. The photo appeared in Howard's book, *Epitaphs for The Living: Words and Images in the Time of AIDS*. Beside the arresting black and white photo in the book is a poem by TPAN's chief founder, Chris Clason.

Embraced by the wind
embracing one another
a minute fragment of the whole
Celebrates
health
participation
unconditional love
The warm glow of aliveness
illuminates the dark
a circle of candles
pooling energy and light
The shadow of a virus
falls flatly at our heels
impotent and useless
attached yet indistinct
Together we are living
with vitality and magnificence
Challenging our fear of intimacy
with the terror of isolation
Recklessly seething
into another bright day
Singing lullabies tenderly
until we sleep

—Chris Clason (1953—1991)

The year before his death, Clason spoke with Bob Hultz. "Death and dying issues are major issues," said Clason. "We have all had to deal with the death of more friends and acquaintances than any of our parents. My parents are in their late 70s, but they have not been exposed to the kind of death that I've been exposed to...It will not be the same for generations after us...It will be better and it will be worse. Just try to maintain the flexibility to handle whatever is coming up. I think death and dying is an important issue, but I think health and living is a very important issue; both deserve equal focus, if not a little extra on health and living issues." (The Chicago LGBT Hall of Fame website).

From *Gay Chicago*. "Paul Wenson died peacefully on April 14, 1989, at the age of 34, from complications due to AIDS. On Sunday, April 23, family and friends released Mr. Wenson's ashes to the universe among a swirl of balloons and unconditional love at a lakeside memorial service at the Belmont Rocks."

Steve Hickson heard about the Belmont Rocks when he was a senior at Northwestern. "I had a friend who was a year older than me who told me about going to this place, the Belmont Rocks. He said he went there one evening and met someone, and then they just started making out right there. I couldn't believe there was a place where it was okay to make out with another guy outdoors like that.

"It wasn't until a year later, in 1989, that I started going to the Rocks myself. I would go with one or two friends, and we would bring our blanket. We would sit and gab and absorb the sun. There was a lot to see at the Rocks. It felt unbelievable because all you had to do was just sit there and watch, and all these gorgeous gay guys would be running around in swimsuits.

"That period was an important part of my life—going from the friends I had being on the same dorm floor, college friends, to finding friends that I had more in common with in the larger world. The Belmont Rocks were a big part of that. I loved going there with my friend, Jim. Some days we would go there and gab the entire time, and other days we might just lie there, and each read our books all day."

The late Nancy Reiff and friends enjoy the sunshine. Photo Courtesy of Brian Wiley.

❖ ❖ ❖

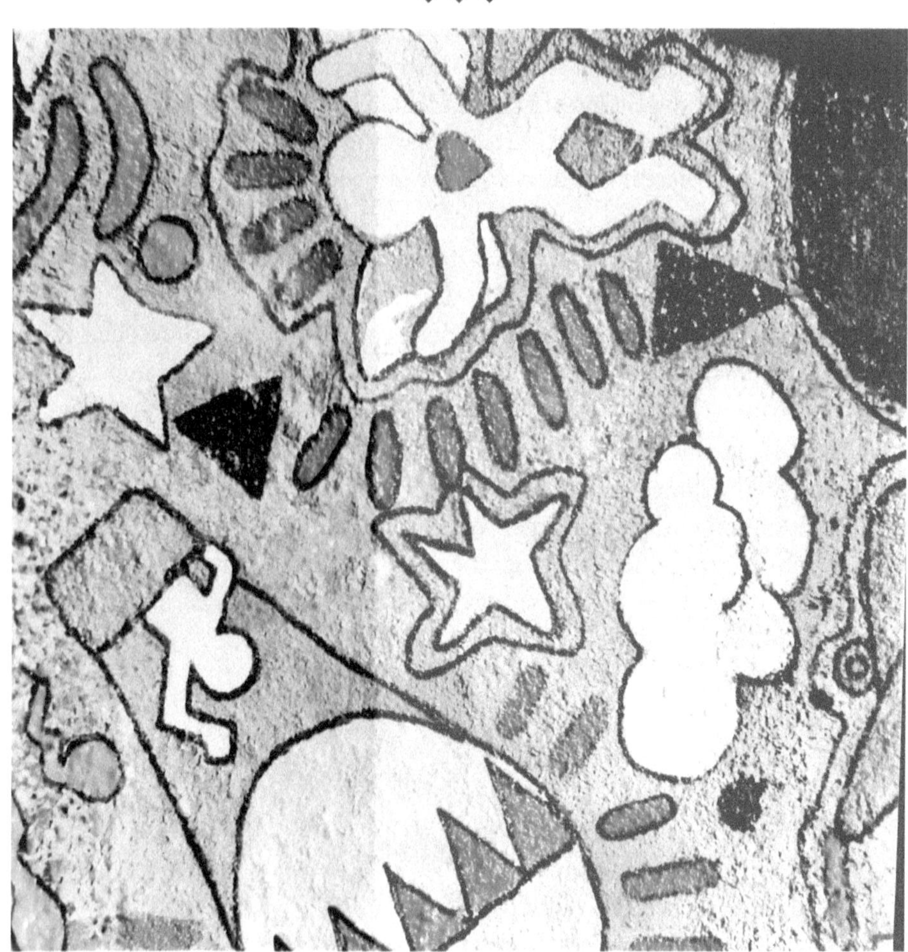

Keith Haring inspired artwork on the Belmont Rocks. Photo courtesy of Bill M.

"I remember the art there," said Adam Kozik. "Some Keith Haring-inspired things, some slogans...one said Don't Give Up—which was a very powerful statement for me to see at the time. There was a lot of poetry and most of the art conveyed an immediate message. The art was always present and always changing, so it was this evolving gallery show as more and more people chose to express themselves through paint or words. It was powerful.

"The Belmont Rocks was our peaceful Stonewall," added Kozik, who first went to the Rocks in 1989 at age 19. "I went there through the early 1990s, and then I relocated to New York. I grew up in the northwest suburbs of Chicago and had been coming into the city alone on the train since I was 16."

By 1989, Kozik was living in Lakeview at Wellington and Broadway. "I remember going to the Belmont Rocks and thinking, this is paradise. The place was just so powerful. I used to bring a book and watch others, and eventually I made friends and met people. There were a lot of regulars there. The Rocks were a great place to meet people. I met a couple of boyfriends there. Anytime you went, day or night, it was exciting to be there, to be out in the open—a place to feel free and feel safe. It was a place to get together that wasn't a bar, and there was a special magic there."

Kozik added, "We need a place to claim and create as our own again. It's entirely possible."

❖ ❖ ❖

Former Carol's Speakeasy and Christopher Street bartender Jeff Pool at the Belmont Rocks. Photo courtesy of Jeff Pool.

❖ ❖ ❖

Boomer had heard about the Rocks, but when he went there, he was less than impressed. "Crab grass, the big rocks, you couldn't wade in the water, and it was dangerous to swim... but for its time, it was magical. The Belmont Rocks was a space we had claimed. The Rocks was a rotten beach, but the importance and daring of the place was in its even being there.

"There were always new people there, but they didn't feel like strangers because we were connected, but there was no secret handshake or anything. You just went, put down your towel, and that was it. Beautifully simple.

"At a time of AIDS and with everything going on, it was important to dare to still be sexy and to look at others with lust, to not let the times take that away. In the face of people getting sick and people dying, it was also important to go there and lie in the sun in a Speedo, maybe even with cock ring on.

"A few times, I saw groups tossing ashes into the Lake at the Rocks. Those gatherings were not about grief. They were celebrations of life. No black suits and ties, and no black crepe. What I saw and heard at all of them were balloons and music and food—it was a party, and they wanted to have that last party at the Rocks."

Malone Sizelove met Nilson, his first boyfriend, at the Belmont Rocks in 1989. "He came up and sat down next to me. He is from Brazil, and his opening line was, 'So where's the joint?' I didn't know if he meant pot or where the gay bars were. He meant pot. So, we talked for a while and then went back to my place. We were together for three years, and he is still my best friend.

"Once I had a lover, I didn't go there [the Rocks]. I remember there being a diversity of people at the Rocks. I would go there on weekends during the day when I was still living in the neighborhood. I remember the gun club being there and thinking that we are fearless to have our recreation area right beside a place with live ammo, especially given the times."

Malone went to the Rocks at night only a few times. "The first time was by accident. I was riding by on my bike and wondered, since so many people cruised there during the day, what it was like at night. All the activity, as far as I could tell, was more on the grass, unless there was a full moon. There were no lights out there, nothing, just the moon and stars and lots of guys walking around shirtless. The Rocks themselves were too tough to negotiate in the darkness. Sometimes it was so dark you couldn't see faces, just shirtless torsos walking around."

❖ ❖ ❖

The crowd begins to gather at the Belmont Rocks. Photo courtesy of Marty Hyams.

❖ ❖ ❖

Mark Blue moved to Lakeview from the south suburbs in 1989. Once settled, he started exploring the local gay scene. "I lived right at Melrose and the Lake. I think I heard about the Belmont Rocks from my neighbors who were going there. I was from the suburbs. I was 30, so I had some experience, but being gay in the city was much different than being gay in the suburbs at the time. This was much more 'out' than the suburbs, where everyone mostly snuck around. At the Rocks, some of the guys on the rocks near the water were naked, and that freaked me out."

Despite his surprise, Blue returned.

At the time, Pete Singer lived downtown, so he didn't venture to the Rocks as frequently, but like Blue, he was an avid bike rider. "I remember the day we met—May 8, 1993. It was a Saturday afternoon and one of those first nice spring days, 80 degrees, and everyone was out. We were both out riding our bikes and we went to the Rocks. There was a walk-a-thon going on along the lakefront, and as it turns out, it was a Right To Life, anti-abortion walk-a-thon, and they had one of their water stops along the bike path at the Belmont Rocks. Clearly, the organizers knew nothing about the route. There were all these families and kids walking, and then on the grass and the Rocks were hundreds of gay men in Speedos. Mark and I were both sitting on the top row of the Rocks watching all this. We both found the whole thing funny. We were flirting a little from a distance. He had his baseball cap on backwards, and I thought he was so cute. Mark is more the extrovert and I am more the introvert. But finally, I knew I just had to say something, so I went up to him and we started talking and ended up going to get something to eat at the Checkers burger place that used to be at Addison and N. Halsted. That was our first date."

"And the rest is history," laughed Blue, "We have been together for 31 years, and in September [2024] we will celebrate being married for 11 years. And it all started at the Belmont Rocks."

Singer added, "After we were together, we would go sunbathing there. Later on, we took our dogs to the Belmont Rocks all the time. The Belmont Rocks was a fond reflection on our life in Chicago. The Rocks could be a place to socialize, or it could be a pick-up place. For us, it was the place where we built a large part of our lives together—our family with our home and our dogs."

Mike Brotebeck moved to Chicago in 1989. By the end of the year, he had met his group of friends, lovingly referred to as the Coven. "That was the name of our group, or what we called ourselves. We were just a bunch of intelligent and witty gay men who liked to get together to laugh and have some fun and be silly. We were always giggling.

"Starting in the spring and summer of 1990, we rode our bikes there. We brought music and food. We always got the same area in the grass. We did that every Saturday in the early years, sometimes on Sunday too. Drinking wasn't really involved in being there, not for me. It was about hanging out with friends, socializing, cruising, and getting into the water. We would usually be

1980s. Mike Brotebeck at the Belmont Rocks. Photo courtesy of Mike Brotebeck.

1980s. Group photo at the Belmont Rocks. Photo courtesy of Mike Brotebeck.

there for a few hours and then make plans for what we were doing that night, which often meant Sidetrack [3349 N. Halsted] followed by Vortex [3631 N. Halsted] or Manhole [3458 N. Halsted]. Some Sunday afternoons, we went to Roscoe's [3354-56 N. Halsted] afterwards, or we would have a barbecue or party at someone's house.

"We did that until probably 1994-1995. For a good five years, that was just a part of life. The community felt pretty tight back in the day. The Rocks was a fun and secure place to socialize, laugh, be in the community, and let loose however you wanted to."

Paul Fairchild came to Chicago in 1990 with his partner, Fred. The couple moved into a place on Waveland and Lake Shore Drive. They had a dog that Fairchild enjoyed walking along the lakefront. "That was how I found the Belmont Rocks. I stumbled upon them by accident. All of a sudden, I looked around and thought, 'Oh my god, look at all these beautiful men.' The artwork on the Rocks was mostly pretty, bright, and vibrant. There was a lot of Keith Haring that I'm sure he didn't do, but it was also a lot of Johnny Loves Steve kind of thing."

Fairchild's favorite memory of the Belmont Rocks was going there for the After Pride Party with his friend Renae Ogletree. "That was extraordinary. I did not expect to see so many families. I remember Vernita [Gray] and Coop running around. The whole place smelled like pot and meat. Everyone was grilling something. This was a community that I had never seen at Pride before. That was my favorite time there, and I went every year after that with Renae."

Drag In for Votes was a documentary feature on Joan Jett Blakk's 1990 campaign for Mayor of Chicago as the Queer Nation candidate. A portion of the 1-hour 29-minute film shows Blakk campaigning, cavorting, and handshaking for votes at the Belmont Rocks.

The documentary was the work of co-directors Gabriel Gomez and Elspeth Kydd. Though co-director Gomez was never personally a fan of the Belmont Rocks, he explained why the Rocks were used for the shoot. "The whole point of the Joan Jett Blakk campaign was to create publicity stunts," said Gomez. "Put Joan in front of an enthusiastic audience, have her look great and say something sensational; that was the strategy to create events, one perfected in the Trump campaign. We picked the Rocks because it was gay and free."

Gomez recalled that it was not too crowded at the Rocks the day of the shoot. "But we had the diehard sunbathing gays." Gomez added that his favorite part of the shoot was that Joan was so comfortable there. "That was a big thing back then, before drag went mainstream. Some rock dwellers really enjoyed Joan, and that made it comfortable and fun, and just as importantly, no one showed her any anger or animosity."

Joe Wright moved to Chicago from St. Louis in 1991, and although he still lived a ways to the north, he periodically rode his bike along the lakefront to the Belmont Rocks. "I never went there for sex," Wright explained. "I went to the Rocks for social reasons.

"My experience there was mostly with the Radical Faeries and the gatherings they had at the Belmont Rocks. There would be gatherings at night at the Rocks. Drumming circles. Ritual Wicca mixed with some New Age things. Wiccan in nature, meaning that meetings with the group often included calling the elements. Nothing bad ever happened, nor was anything bad called for. This was all good and protective magic. Some of those evenings, the area out by the Rocks became queer faerie witch time."

Wright continued, "Usually about eight or more would show up, but others would be drawn to the loose chaos...that concept of structure without structure is an element of Wicca. I think the gatherings were based upon the lunar cycle and were also dependent upon the weather. The gatherings were faerie-based, so anyone might show up, not just gay men. Being there was beautiful, to experience peace, calm, stability, and chaos. Chicago was an intense place in the 1990s, and these events at the Rocks were always so calming."

One of the peculiarities of the Belmont Rocks was its proximity to the Lincoln Park Gun Club. Many of those who frequented the Rocks can recall the periodic pop of gunfire, and if the wind was right, it was not uncommon for a sunbather or two at the south end of the Rocks to be pelted by bits of skeet.

The Lincoln Park Gun Club was built in 1912 by a collection of prominent Chicagoans, including Oscar Mayer and P.K. Wrigley. The Gun Club had been polluting Lake Michigan for over half a century when, in 1970, Casey Bukro, Environmental Editor for *The Chicago Tribune,* wrote, "The Lincoln

Park Gun Club has been ordered by the state to stop polluting Lake Michigan with clay pigeon fragments and other debris."

The debris complaint came in a letter from the Illinois Sanitary Water board about the round plastic shotcups from shotgun shells that were being blown into the water when club members shot clay pigeons over the water.

"...In addition, we are informed that almost one million rounds of ammunition are fired yearly at this club, with the result that over 50,000 pounds of lead and one million clay pigeons and shotcups are discharged into Michigan each year,' said the letter.

"In answer to the complaint about fragments falling into the lake, [Gun Club President] Seymour Silver said he will get a letter from the Winchester

Looking south at the Belmont Rocks with the Lincoln Park Gun Club in the distance. Author's collection.

Firearms company showing that the clay pigeons are made of inert material.

"'Since they are inert, they cause no pollution problem,'" said Silver. [Burko, 'Gun Club is Cited for Pollution,' *The Chicago Tribune*, June 16, 1970].

Two decades passed before action was taken against the gun club. As *The Chicago Tribune* reported on April 25, 1991, in the news item, 'Clock starts ticking on revoked permit for Lincoln Park Gun Club.'

"The Lincoln Park Gun Club was formally notified Wednesday morning that its permit to operate a skeet and trap shooting range in Lincoln Park would be cancelled in 30 days.

"'We have given them a 30-day notice to terminate the permit,' said Chicago Park District President Richard Devine. 'After that, they will have no legal right to fire weapons in the park.'

"…The notification stated that club members should remove their personal property from the facility before midnight May 24, when the permit cancellation becomes effective."

Following the closure and after two years of renovation, the space was repurposed and reopened by the Park District.

Cameron McWhirter of *The Chicago Tribune* wrote of the newly renovated space. "The Chicago Park District is set Friday to open the former Lincoln Park Gun Club as a revamped visitor's center, complete with a bicycle shop, a food stand, and a sign declaring no shooting allowed."

"…For decades, gun aficionados unloaded round after round of lead at clay pigeons hurled over the lake. A few yards in the opposite direction, bikers, walkers, and joggers traveled a park path next to Lake Shore Drive.

"But a fight over the gun club's right to remain on the site broke out five years ago. The battle pitted shooters in a club that had been around for decades against angry park protectors who were tired of the noise, the potential danger, and possible environmental hazards.

"After three years of wrangling, the Park District voted in 1991 to terminate the lease and take over the property. And the gun club, after losing its clubhouse and facing potential liability for polluting the lakeshore, disbanded. Once the dust settled, the Park District found a lot of work ahead and an expensive controversy over the legacy of birdshot.

"Enough lead for a Civil War battle, about 400 tons, has accumulated on the muddy lake bottom. The Environmental Protection Agency is now testing the waters for lead contamination. If the lead poses a long-term health threat, it will have to be removed, with the Park District possibly picking up the tab.

"…Also, thousands of shattered clay pigeons were embedded in 2 acres of topsoil. The contaminated soil had to be carted off at a cost to the district of about $500,000. Roughly 2,400 truckloads of soil were brought in as fill."

The Chicago Tribune coverage continued with explanations for the ongoing expense of cleanup as well as the repurposing of the clubhouse by the Park District, "with meeting rooms and offices for neighborhood groups, including runners' clubs and bicycling groups, and is accessible to the physically disabled."

Hours for the center are 10 a.m. to 8 p.m. daily. (McWhirter, 'Onetime gun club has gone green as Chicago Park District takes over,' *The Chicago Tribune*, May 28, 1993).

The visitor's center in the repurposed gun club building was short-lived. Four years later, in the early morning hours of September 2, 1997, the former Lincoln Park Gun Club fell to the wrecking ball courtesy of the Chicago Park District. The 76-year-old clubhouse building that had been part of the landscape of the Belmont Rocks for decades was now a heap of splintered wood, shattered glass, and assorted debris.

After moving to Chicago in 1992, Mitchell Fain stayed with a girlfriend in a studio apartment at Melrose and Lake Shore. However, it was not until the following spring that Fain discovered the Belmont Rocks. "It was one of those really nice days early in the year, April or May, when the weather is nice and all of gay Chicago pops out. I was out running and discovered the Rocks. It was completely organic and just like Dorothy going from sepia tone to color. I saw a couple of guys there and then another couple.

"That first time I went, I didn't even know how to cruise." Fain continued, "I came from a small town, and all I had to go by was something from *Longtime Companion* about turning and looking three times. And I saw a cute guy at the Rocks, and he did that. He stopped and turned, and so I did the same, and we eyed each other again. Then it was three times, just like in the movie. Cruising was a success. I had my first hookup in Chicago that day."

For the first several months he lived in Chicago, Fain had only straight friends. Discovering the Rocks opened him to another world. "I was always a sex positive person, and I could not believe that this place was right across the street." When Fain went to the Rocks, he tended to go during the week. "The weekend crowd at the Rocks was more intimidating.

"My friend Byron and I would go to the Rocks to have what Byron termed, 'a dick stretch.'" Fain explained, "That meant you flirt and get excited, a little aroused, then you cool down, then play around a little, get excited again—that was having a dick stretch. And we did that at the Rocks. When it came to that sort of thing, it felt like the Rocks freed us from the darkness, literally. It was an outside alternative to dark rooms, to dark bars, to the shadows...the Belmont Rocks took cruising out of the dark and put it into the day in a safe way. We were in the middle of the city on the lip of this beautiful lake, and in this place where being gay wasn't a problem.

This page and top of next, examples of art on the Belmont Rocks. Photo courtesy of Bruce Dunlop.

Woman painting on the rocks. Photo courtesy of Janice Polito.

"I also remember the bohemian artwork," added Fain. "I always had an appreciation for public art, but I only knew of government belmont-sanctioned public art—like a statue in a park, or a mural in the post office, that kind of thing. This public art was very different. It was a beautiful, eclectic art of both words and images, with a good amount of graffiti. The art there had energy. There was chalk and painting, and carving. Everything. The art on the Rocks was an organic art explosion—some very sophisticated and some exquisitely primitive. It was free artistic expression. Looking back, losing all the art is almost the saddest part to me."

Artwork covered many of the limestone slabs, making the area a queer open-air gallery. Some carved the names of loved ones in the stones. The Rocks were our tablets. The art on display included everything from elaborate murals and vibrant geometric designs to painted love poems, personal symbols, and initials carved inside a heart.

Many LGBTQ folks had been silenced or unseen their entire lives—this opportunity for expression was an important part of the Belmont Rocks. The artwork was another means of expressing the freedom that was central to the place.

Walking the length of the Rocks and viewing the artwork meant taking in assorted queer voices and points of view—playful and sexy, wildly artistic, definitely political, highly romantic, and often deeply poetic. The artwork was always fading and ever-changing. With exposure to the waves and wind along Lake Michigan, much of the painted art only lasted a few seasons. Some of the chalk art only remained until the next hard rain or the next crashing cycle of big waves.

From 1977 until 2001, the Belmont Rocks was the site of the After Pride party, a celebration in the park for those who felt excluded from the North Halsted bar scene—primarily LGBTQ People of Color. The After Pride party was a celebratory dance party with food and entertainment, plenty of music, and a lot of dancing. The party also became a major site for HIV testing, women's health information, voter registration, reproductive rights, and various forms of community outreach.

"We were the ones who started things," said Pat McCombs. "Harriet Robinson and I decided to have a party there after the parade. People wanted to party in the neighborhood, and a lot of people didn't want to go all the way back to the South Side for a party, so we had it there. No permits or anything. The lesbians just took over. We did our own thing. We didn't want to go to that rally down in the park that was after the parade. Instead, we just told people, 'Hey, we're having a barbecue at the Belmont Rocks.' I had Executive Sweet at the time, so

I had plenty of contacts." [Executive Sweet hosted parties for professional and working Women of Color to socialize and network in a safe environment].

McCombs continued, "We set up in the grass closer to the parking lot. After that first year, the After Party just grew and grew. At some point, it got more official, and Bob Yeaworth got involved, and other people got involved, and we all just chipped in the money to get the port-a-johns—we lesbians called them port-a-janes. Then there were DJs, and the party grew. More guys came to the party, and the drag queens came to the party, and it just kept getting bigger every year. There was plenty of food—you know, Black folks and cooking. There were grills and tents set up, and people selling food. I hardly ever went to the parade after we started doing that party. I was busy setting up the tent and getting things ready during the parade. I used to do massages there, too."

McCombs suspects that at some point, some of the yacht club people complained. "The element of the party changed, and it could get wild. I think the yacht club people ignored it for a long time because it was only one day a year that we would take over, but finally, they had enough. We didn't have permits or anything like that. By moving the After Pride party to Montrose, the city actually did us a favor because it is so much bigger and the party got a board and sponsors and all that."

In her biography the late lesbian activist and community pioneer Vernita Gray (1948-2014) recalled the After Pride parties at the Belmont Rocks, "For many gay men, it really became about putting on your peacock feathers and coming out. So, we lesbians were like, well—we don't know if we really want to do this with the gay men, so we went to the Belmont Rocks with our potlucks and our families and our boom boxes.

"The roots of that were women wanting to do something separate from gay men, but at the same time, it was all about gay day and having a celebration. The boys wanted to all get naked and do each other, and we all wanted to have a potluck and have a barbecue and get out our boom boxes."

Gray continued, "The person who really changed the Belmont Rocks party was a gay man, and that was Sam Davis. He was an attorney and had some money, and one year he brought out music and put speakers up, and that was the year, unfortunately, that the police sent the horses in, and really ruined our party at the Belmont Rocks and scared people and made them leave. We came back the next year. After that, we started having to get permits to be in the park, and before, when it was just lesbians, nobody bothered us." (Baim, Keehnen. *Vernita Gray: From Woodstock to the White House*, Prairie Avenue Productions, 2014).

The After Party at the Rocks changed when entrepreneur and attorney Samuel F. Davis Jr. [d. 1993] and his business partner and lover Bob Yeaworth [d. 2020] entered the picture. The duo had opened several gay bars in Chicago, including Dëeks [3401 N. Sheffield], Pangea [3209 N. Halsted], and the Clubhouse [440 N. Halsted]. Each of their three venues offered a safe party environment, particularly for Chicago's LGBTQ African American community. When Davis and Yeaworth came in, they helped to turn the After Pride party into a production with proper permits, popular DJs, on-stage entertainment, port-a-potties, and eventually, the police.

June 28, 1987, as reported in *Gay Chicago,* "Chicago police allegedly harass a group of mostly Black gay men and lesbians dancing to the music of DJ Frankie Knuckles at the Belmont Rocks on the evening of the Gay and Lesbian Pride Day."

"I probably went to the Belmont Rocks for the first time in the late 1980s," said Mary Morten. "I was surprised to find that people gathered at the Rocks after the Pride Parade. There was a great vibe there, so that became what we did after the parade. People were cooking out, and some people set up tents. There was music and games, dancing, and lots of socializing.

"I would see people at that party that I would never see anywhere else. Everyone was having a great time, but standing there, I had to put on my organizer cap and think, where are all these people during the week? There were hundreds of people there who I never saw anywhere else. It was important that we be able to reach people and contact people when we need things like legislative support. By the mid-1990s, there was much more organizing going on there—HIV, voter registration, and a real connecting of communities."

Morten added, "Once we got settled and the food was put out, there was the music and the dancing. I love to dance. Those were the best things—dancing and seeing people I did not see anyplace else, and for that time we were all together."

"While I did not hang out at the Rocks or our other Chicago beaches much, I loved covering the Rocks parties for Black Pride events. People from all over the city would come to the Rocks (and later to Montrose) to celebrate, listen to great music, and just hang out for Pride. It was a rare time when African Americans felt comfortable in what were usually mostly white spaces, and a time to show the true diversity of our community."—Tracy Baim, cofounder, *Windy City Times*

"I first went to the Rocks in 1985 when I moved north," said Sanford Gaylord. "I was living on Grace and found out the place to go and see other Black gays. I remember the After Pride parties at the Rocks and Frankie Knuckles spinning there for free. I remember him playing Teddy Pendergrass' 'You Can't Hide from Yourself.' People were parking their cars along Lake Shore Drive. They were getting tickets on their cars, but people didn't seem to care. The music called you. When you heard the boom boom boom of the music, you got excited. The music had life. Someone was always playing House Music there. Dancing in the park was a whole new experience. I had that experience before in clubs, but not right out in the daylight.

"I loved going there and seeing friends, but the After Party was also bittersweet because you would ask about people who weren't there, and sometimes you would find out they had passed away or were sick and soon to pass. That was the downside."

Gaylord added that he chose to focus on the joy at the Rocks, "The happy times. Those were some magnificent moments in life."

Brian Kirst was a young blonde, and blue-eyed twink from a small town in New York with a population of 600. "I was so naïve. The first time I went to the Rocks was in 1989. I was going to DePaul at the time and was sneaking into the bars. I was in Christopher Street [3458 N. Halsted] and I met this handsome, muscular older man named Scott. I'm 99% sure he was the one who took me to the Rocks the first time. I had not really felt immersed in the community. The Belmont Rocks were a way to connect—a gay beach and a cruising spot as well.

"After that, I remember going there specifically to try and pick someone up. I didn't know how to do it. I mostly went there alone, so I brought my book and tried to see what cruising was all about. I remember one 'almost' encounter there with an older guy in a Speedo with a very big package. I was too nervous to do anything, but the scene was very erotically charged. I was turned on by the experience, but I just couldn't."

By the early 1990s, Kirst was working in an office downtown as well as volunteering for several organizations, specifically Stop AIDS and NARAL Chicago (National Abortion Rights Action League). Kirst also reflected on his volunteer work at the Belmont Rocks.

"I was eager...determined to make a difference...and was willing to take on almost any reasonable thing that these two important activist groups requested of me. Once or twice, I was asked to visit the Belmont Rocks during the summer months to drop off handouts on safer sex practices and to get the various sun worshippers there to sign whatever petition the powers-that-be at Stop AIDS needed help with at the moment.

"As I hopped off the L train in my dress shirt and tie to pick up my materials from the head office that first time, it did cross my mind that maybe someone's day at the beach was not the proper time to remind them about the pandemic that was decimating our community—we all need a break from reality, after all. But I was raised to respect my elders and those in charge...you know, obey the school principal, kneel before the priest, apologize to the neighborhood lady when I took the apples that littered her yard without permission—that sort of thing...so if the powers-that-be wanted work done at a huge LGBTQIA gathering spot, who was I to argue?

"Sweating freely in my professional attire, I headed over to the lake and climbed up and down and over and around, pacing back and forth upon the stony tiers that made up our gay version of the Washington Monument, trying to educate and inform. I'm sure there were many that gladly scribbled their signatures on my clipboard, secured documents, and gracefully shoved whatever literature I offered them into their overflowing beach bags.

"But what I remember the most was the skinny, neon thong-wearing men who were furious at me for interrupting their blissful day off, confirming my original fear. 'This is not the time and the place,' they would hiss at me and turn onto their stomachs, ignoring my soft, embarrassed apologies. Still, I kept on with my assigned task, sometimes retreating to the head of the rocks to catch people before they disrobed and settled in, sometimes just moving much further down the cliff-like pyramids, removing myself from anyone's offended sightline.

"Now, decades later, I find I have such bittersweet affection for those angry men who hissed at my intrusions. I hope they are alive still and happy, but I have a feeling some are not, that they have succumbed to the disease that I was trying so eagerly to warn them about long, long ago. What they could have taught me, huh? But I also have that same sense of compassion and sympathy for myself. I can almost picture myself then, hot and rumpled…my work shoes pinching my feet, hoisting myself from ledge to ledge, trying so hard to be of service, fucking up…totally misreading body language at times, but wanting so, so badly to do good even as those mid-evening waves and the carefree laughter of those warm month revelers lapped all around me."

Don Bell did outreach at the After Pride festivities, first with Stop AIDS and then with Howard Brown. "For Stop AIDS and Howard Brown, we made up safe sex packets with information to distribute. All the different organizations would table on the west side of Lake Shore Drive. The Parade would end down in the park, and then everyone would walk north on the path, and there would be everyone tabling—distributing information, doing outreach, and recruiting volunteers. Howard Brown, Stop AIDS, Test Positive Aware, Horizons, the Names Project … Social organizations, like Black and White Men Together, were tabling and distributing information as well. There was an enormous amount of outreach. Then, after you went by the organization tables, you went beneath the underpass to the festival at the Rocks. I had a chance to cross to the festival and see what was happening, but I was there to volunteer."

In 1997, Keith Butler moved to Chicago. The same year, he went to the After Pride party at the Belmont Rocks for the first time. "There was barbecuing. The music was pumping. There was partying and some pot smoking, too. It was like we could march in the Pride Parade together, but the parties afterwards were almost segregated. I went to the After Party for a few years. I didn't go to the After Party if I was dating someone. If I were, we would go to the parade and then go have dinner or go home."

Butler added that he is happy to see the AIDS Garden Chicago now in the area that was formerly the Rocks. "I'm happy it's there as a way to honor memories, but I am also happy it is there as more of a guarantee that the area won't get destroyed and that it will be there for a while to honor the place and what it meant to so many people."

In 2001, the After Pride event at the Belmont Rocks was relocated to Montrose Harbor. According to reports, the reasoning was that having the North Halsted Street pride aftermath and the After Party at the Rocks happening simultaneously in the same precinct was stretching the police force too thin.

Afternoon get together at the Rocks. Photo by David Klein.

In 2001, Karen Hawkins covered the relocation of the After Pride party for *Windy City Times*.

"In response to concerns about public safety, the Belmont Rocks celebration is moving to Montrose beach, ending a decades-long tradition in the area.

"The day-long event, held on Pride Sunday and predominantly attended by Blacks and Latinos, is a gay institution for many in the community and draws thousands of people from around the country.

"But despite a history of law and order, organizer Michael O'Connor said area officials have decided the event is a public safety hazard and has to go.

"'It's such a strain on the whole neighborhood to have it all in the same area,' said Ald. Bernie Hansen, whose district includes the Pride parade and Belmont Rocks. 'It's just too much of a drain.' Hansen said that no events will be allowed at the Belmont Harbor area on Sunday, and that a command post will be set up notifying people that the Rocks event has been moved.

"While O'Connor acknowledges that the new space is bigger and better suited to the event's needs, he doesn't feel that a command post on the day of the event is enough. He is calling on Hansen and the police department to launch an advertising campaign to get the word out. 'We will move,' O'Connor said. 'For us, the issue there is a fun-filled day on the lakefront celebrating our cultural diversity.'

"'We don't advertise (now), because we don't have to,' he added.

"O'Connor said Rocks organizers had already secured a Park District permit for the Belmont area when officials told them to move. He said the event will go on as planned unless the community indicates it wants otherwise.

"'It's not at Belmont unless the community wants to fight,' he said." (Hawkins, 'Belmont Rocks to Move Pride' from the May 2, 2001, *Windy City Times*).

Six weeks later, Hawkins penned a follow-up piece, 'Belmont Rocks Battle Continues as City Moves Event to Montrose.' (*Windy City Times*, June 20, 2001).

"Though the city and police department are set in their decision to move the 20-year-plus Belmont Rocks celebration to Montrose Harbor, some GLBT activists have said they intend to stand their ground at Belmont.

"...In early May, officials, citing concerns about public safety, announced that the event was moving.

"'It's such a strain on the whole neighborhood to have it all in the same area,' said Ald. Bernie Hansen, whose ward includes the Pride parade and Belmont Rocks. 'It's just too much of a drain.'

"In a letter dated Aug. 17, 2000, Hansen urges Park District General Superintendent David Doig not to issue permits for 'events at any park in my ward the day of the Gay Pride Parade that are not directly related to the parade itself. ...These events draw unruly and raucous people into the neighborhood who have shown a blatant disregard for the residents of my ward and their property.'

"However, in January of this year, Belmont Rocks Coordinating Committee President Michael O'Connor was given a permit for the Rocks, leading Hansen to again write to Doig.

"In a Jan. 17, 2001, letter, Hansen chastises Doig for issuing the permit and says, 'I hope I do not have to pursue alternative avenues to prevent this group from again wreaking havoc on our neighborhood.'

"Hansen indicates in the letter that 23rd District Police Commander Richard Guerrero agrees with him on the matter.

"By late March, O'Connor had received a revised park district permit, this one for Montrose Harbor.

"O'Connor and others have taken issue with Hansen's depiction of the crowds at the Rocks as 'unruly and raucous.'

"'There is nothing in the police record to indicate that any of this is true,' O'Connor said. 'I question his accusation. Who is he talking about?'

"Hansen said in May that a command post will be set up notifying people that the Rocks event has been moved. The parking lot at Belmont will be closed and used as a staging area for the day's events, though the land south of the staging area will be open for picnics.

"According to a city release, Montrose Harbor offers 'improved access, expanded parking, more spaces for picnics, additional public conveniences, nearby beach facilities and a playground for children.'

"While O'Connor is upset with the way the move was carried out—without input from the Belmont Rocks Coordinating Committee—he said his focus is to make the most of the day.

"'All I want to do is make sure we have a fun-filled day at Montrose Beach,' he said. 'We'll deal with (the political situation) on June 25.'

"Others in the community, however, reportedly aren't as willing to make concessions. People who spoke on the condition of anonymity said they intend to test the city's stated openness to having Belmont open to picnics. They said they're going to set up at Belmont as they always have and see how they are treated by the police.

"There are those among them who believe that racism, not public safety, ultimately fueled the move to Montrose.

"'It's unfortunate that the police...are trying to resegregate Belmont Rocks,' O'Connor said.

In 2024, longtime community activist Michael O'Connor recalled the incident. "They came in with riot troops, on horses and with shields. Nobody wanted any violence. They made Frankie Knuckles shut the music down, and then they cleared us out. They said we needed a park permit.

"After we got kicked out of Belmont, we said, no more. We have to deal with this. We have to have all the proper park permits so they cannot do that to us again. Once we applied for the permit, that's when all the trouble started with [44th Ward Alderman] Bernie Hansen."

O'Connor continued, "Helen Schiller of the 49th Ward said, 'Come to Montrose Harbor, it's a bigger area and I'll help with the permits.' There were a number of people who helped make sure the transition to Montrose Harbor went smoothly and all the proper paperwork was done. At first, I wanted to sue as a reaction to the overt racism. If this party had been going on in Jackson Park, there would be no problem. There was a panic because some Black people decided not to self-segregate, and Chicago is a very segregated city.

"The parade attracted a lot of different people than gay white men," added O'Connor. "They were all in the park. Men, women, and trans—everybody was out there. My favorite was when people would bring their whole families, and I would hear that everyone in the family was having a good time. We didn't have violence. We were there to party. DJs were playing the music. We had a stage set up with acts like Sheri Payne and Otis Mack. There were lots of different entertainers and DJs. We had speakers as well and a market set up. There was voter registration, and there was the Breast Cancer Awareness van.

"The real goal of the After Party was to address some of the health disparities in the Black and Brown communities, especially with HIV and AIDS. I saw that happening with my friends. We were dropping like flies, and you didn't hear a word about it. In one day, we could help thousands, and we did. We made it work. I am so grateful that a lot of people found out their status that day. Knowing and dealing with our status was a major health weakness in communities of color."

❖ ❖ ❖

St Sukie de la Croix remembers. "I moved to Chicago from England in 1991 and soon became aware of the Belmont Rocks as being a gay place to go. I went

Nightspots cover featuring Brian-Mark. Photo St Sukie de la Croix.

there a couple of times, but it was deserted—I suspect it may have passed its heyday by then. As I'm not someone who enjoys lying in the sun, I may have passed it a couple of times, but it was never a destination for me.

"In 2001, I became the managing editor of *Nightspots* magazine—it was taken over later by Kirk Williamson. One thing I wanted to do was always have local people on the cover—who needs another picture of Boy George? So, every week, my team of rebels and I would pick someone for the cover: a bartender, drag queen, lesbian sports team, etc.

"One local I picked for the cover was adult film star Brian-Mark—he had an interesting tattoo on his back that I wanted to photograph. He agreed to do it.

"As much as I wanted to put Brian-Mark full-frontal naked on the cover (he was substantially endowed), the company policy was no poles, no holes.

"I don't know whose idea it was to do the photo shoot at Belmont Rocks, but that's where we ended up. I only wanted to photograph his back tattoo, but while I was fiddling with my camera, Brian-Mark stripped off and was buck-naked.

"I was reminded of a lyric from a Frank Zappa song—'Anything more than a mouthful is wasted.'

"So that's how a topless Brian-Mark appeared on the cover of *Nightspots* magazine with the tattoo saying, 'SEX PIG.'"

Keith Butler was from a small town in Virginia when he came to visit Chicago in 1990 at the age of 17. "I knew I was gay, but had no experience or ideas of what that meant. I came to visit my uncle and his roommate Richard, who, of course, was very obvious to me that they were a lot more than just roommates.

"One day, I decided to take a bike ride from North Sheridan to as far as I thought I could go. On this ride, I really took in the city and the people. I saw the beauty of it all and knew for sure that I was no longer in Windsor, Virginia. As I rode, I felt this sense of joy and comfort. I felt for the first time in a long time that I was ok."

Butler continued, "I came to a point in my ride where the lake, which to me looked like the ocean from back home, was so beautiful that I had to stop and really appreciate it. As I sat looking at the lake and listening to my cassette tape Walkman, I was overcome with a sense of peace and belonging. It was not long before I saw a man walk by me wearing nothing but a jockstrap, and I was like, what the ???. I was thinking to myself, people are allowed to walk around like that here. Wow!"

Following that surprise, Butler witnessed something even more shocking. "I looked down a few steps from where I was sitting to see that another man was standing there naked, and I thought to myself, I really must have died and gone to heaven. Where was I? I could not believe a place like this existed or that it was even possible to be this free. Could I ever be that free?"

Returning from his ride, Butler asked his uncle and Richard about what he had seen.

"I was then informed that the place was the Belmont Rocks. I was told this was the place where gay men could be free to be themselves and find others to converse with, sunbathe, or cruise to make sexual connections. As they said this, I was reminded that it was located in the place where I found the lake to be so beautiful. So, for a little Black teenager from Virginia that had no experiences to speak of until then, I had indeed found heaven, and for the rest of my stay that visit, I made sure to visit the Belmont Rocks often."

Greg O'Neill first went to the Belmont Rocks in 1992. "I had just moved here from North Carolina after I graduated from business school. One day, a friend who lived here said, 'Let's go to the beach.' So we went to the Rocks. When we got there, I thought this is not a beach. Where's the sand? This beach was a gathering of mostly men. Everybody brought their towels, and they were spread out all over. It looked like an insta-party.

"Going to the Rocks was a good way to get socialized into the community and meet people. Sometimes I would meet up with others. Four or five of us would go there and hang out and cruise guys. An early Chicago friend of mine had his 30th birthday party there. He had a picnic day at the Rocks with potluck food and cocktails. It was a birthday party, but it organically grew into this spontaneous larger party. People brought friends, and they joined the group."

O'Neill also liked to bike to the Rocks on his own. "I would bring a sandwich, some sunscreen, find a flat rock, have my lunch, and check out the vibe there. I was an afternoon Rocks guy, so I would get there later if I had the full day and stay until late afternoon, and sometimes even until dusk. As it got darker, especially in the heat of summer, the flies and gnats there could be bad. During the week, if I rode my bike to work, I would stop off at the Rocks on my way home.

"I knew the Army Corps of Engineers needed to redo the shoreline, but it was still sad watching it happen. It was the end of an era, even if I understood why it needed to happen. A lot of people were very emotional about it. They had been going there for years. They had memories of people who were gone. It was tough to lose the Belmont Rocks, but that was the reality. And the gay community in Chicago just keeps morphing and changing."

❖ ❖ ❖

In 1994, a scene from the independent lesbian romance, *Go Fish,* was filmed at the Belmont Rocks. The groundbreaking feature was directed by Rose Troche, starred Guinevere Turner, and was written by the two as well. The Chicago-shot film also starred V.S. Brodie.

Two years earlier, the gay adult romance, *Baby, It's You,* directed by Toby Ross and starring Brad Hunt, included a scene filmed at the Belmont Rocks as well.

❖ ❖ ❖

The waves could get rough along the stone slabs. Photo by Marty Hyams.

Antics at the Belmont Rocks, 1985. Photo courtesy of Norbert Shimkus.

Van Barnes came to Chicago in 1992 and left for New York City the following year. "I came here right out of high school. I came from a small town where I was constantly harassed for being effeminate. I came to Chicago, and when I got here, I ran under the gay umbrella. I wanted to be a part of the community, and since I wasn't of age, the Belmont Rocks was a place to find that, and it was free. I liked going to the Rocks. I felt safe there, or at least safer. Coming from a small town and having been gay bashed, the Rocks seemed safe, sophisticated, and unreal. It was safe to be a noticeable faggot there, but even then, I was still looking over my shoulder.

"At the Belmont Rocks, I mostly people watched, and that was free entertainment. In those days, straight-acting and masculine gay men were the thing, and I was an effeminate, malnourished twink—so I also went there and looked at all the men that I couldn't have. I always ran into people I knew there—lots of nightlife people went there. It was a fun place to go and be scantily clad and maybe sunbathe naked."

In Chicago during the early 1990s, Barnes became a club kid, drag queen, and box dancer by the name of T.J. Mozzarella. "Kinda cheesy but sure to pleasey." Barnes lived across from Roscoe's and performed at places like Shelter/Quench [564 W. Fulton] and Berlin [954 W. Belmont].

Barnes added, "The artist Greer Lankton [1958-1996] made me a pair of rice boobs that I wore to the Rocks and got wet. For a year and a half, Greer modeled her doll, Sissy, with the bald head and the curl, after me. That was her most important doll. Then Sissy became Twiggy and other icons. That doll was always in transition. I dried the rice boobs out after I got them wet, but they still stank. I kept them for years, though. They were an art piece, and they're in a collection today."

Mark Freitas moved to Chicago from Detroit in 1992. Soon after arriving, his friend Steve took him around town and showed him all the important gay spots. "Like the secret jackoff places and other spots of interest. The Belmont Rocks was one of the places. I liked it from the start and ended up going there every week. I liked hanging out on a towel on a nice, gentle summer day and watching the boys hanging out on the grass and the rocks. It was a nice, chill atmosphere. We would get there in the early afternoon and stay for maybe three or four hours.

"Something cool—I have a tattoo on my shoulder of a Mayan skull from Chichen Itza in Mexico, and I found the same image carved on the rocks one day," said Freitas, adding, "The chalk graffiti and images on the Rocks were so colorful. Super colorful. Whole scenes.

"People even wrote their phone numbers on the Rocks in chalk," added Freitas' husband, Doug Sefara, who also moved from Detroit to Chicago in 1992. Despite this coincidence, Frietas and Serafa did not meet until 1996.

Doug Serafa first came to the Belmont Rocks on a visit to Chicago in 1986. "I had friends who had moved to Lakeview and lived near Berlin. They took me to the Rocks. That place felt like its own world, a place on the fringe, like a pocket of San Francisco dropped into the Midwest."

"There was a sense of ownership of the space," added Freitas.

"And there was also a sexual energy to the Rocks," said Serafa, "with guys laying out in very high shorts and swimwear. There was the music."

"I was the queer punk rock boy who drove everyone crazy with his boom box," recalled Freitas. "We also came to the After Pride party at the Rocks.

They had good DJs and set up a proper sound system. Sound is not easy to do outdoors, but it was a real party in the park. I liked it better than the Pride Parade. I still have a T-shirt from one of those parties that says, Help our Horny Friends. It was to help protect the rhinos."

Serafa adds, "Everything moved from the Belmont Rocks and north to Hollywood Beach so quickly—a migration happened from 1995 to 1999. It started with volleyball, and then the attitude was sort of, 'Why go to the Rocks when we can go to a real beach.'"

Brian Wiley was in his early 20s and living at Halsted and Wellington when he discovered the Belmont Rocks. "I came home from my job and the moon was just so bright that I grabbed my cassette Walkman and walked to the lake. I have such a vivid memory of how this beautiful moon ended right at the Rocks. Then a sailboat passed slowly through the moonbeams; it was so picturesque. So, I sat and watched, and then I started to notice that there were more people around, people who were not interested in looking at the moon or the sailboat. I realized I had happened onto a gay hotspot. I was both excited and scared, but I held my ground.

"Half the time I went there to be social and half the time I went there for sex," adds Wiley. "When the gun club had the chain link fence along the rocks that went up to the water, you could hold onto the post and swing around, and there were caves down in front of the gun club caused by erosion, and people would always be fucking around in those during the day. I don't think anybody would risk going in there at night.

"As a sober alternative, the Rocks was a big hangout. I especially would hang out there a lot with my friend Nancy Reiff. We went there due to sobriety and for our love of the sun. She would pick me up in her convertible and we would go to Starbucks and then head to the Rocks for six hours of sun."

Wiley continued, "When the gun club left and the fence and building came down, they made the lakefront more of a continuous parkway. Straight people began coming there. This was around 2000, so Nancy and I did our own bit of activism. We took a stencil with the words QUEER ZONE on it and then the male and female symbols together. Then used pink and purple spray paint to stencil QUEER ZONE every 20-30 feet on the Rocks until the paint ran out. We were remarking our territory. When I heard the Rocks were going to be demolished, I went down there with a chisel and hammer and spent a couple of hours chopping out a bit of the Rocks that had QUEER ZONE stenciled on it. I've had that ever since as a part of the Rocks and as a memory of my friend, Nancy.

"Everyone used to hang out at the Rocks, all types of people and all economic backgrounds. We were all hanging out there," said Wiley. "The Rocks was the great social leveler. It was a place where people could be themselves. For me, that meant the social side and the naughty side. I considered the Rocks a sanctuary. The existence of the Rocks was probably more important in my life than I will ever know."

Why We Went to the Rocks When Chicago has 25 Miles of Beach
By Victoria Elliott

The Belmont Rocks has been primarily thought of as a gay male space, but lesbians, like me, went there too.

My fondest memory of the rocks is one dark night in the late 1980s or early 1990s when the sky was full of thick clouds. I had gone there with Agnes, a woman I was dating. Maybe it was our first date. Perhaps it was our second date? I don't remember. I do remember holding her hand and kissing her. We sat on the hard rocks, hidden from whatever was going on in the park behind us, hidden from the periodic police patrols. We listened to the water lap against the rocks and watched lightning strike the water in the distance.

We had gone out to dinner that night, but even in Lakeview, we did not feel safe being publicly affectionate. We were not in the mood to go to Paris Dance or any of the other lesbian bars. Or maybe we were still under 21? That's also possible, so we went to the rocks where in the dark we felt safe. At the time you almost never saw same-sex couples holding hands even during gay pride in Lakeview.

I whiled away many a Saturday afternoon there after going to Horizons youth group. Sometimes I went on Sunday

It wasn't only men who enjoyed the Rocks. Photo courtesy of Victoria Stagg Elliott.

afternoons. When you're under 21 and don't have money, your options for just hanging out with other gay people are extremely limited. There was Horizons and People Like Us (the gay bookstore) and the Belmont Rocks.

While I sat on the rocks with my friends, we discussed how we—the post-Stonewall generation—were going to change the world. We wanted something better.

I used to always say the same thing, "Chicago has 25 miles of beautiful public beach. Why are we sitting on the rocks?" It felt like an act of rebellious hubris to say, "We deserve better."

We sat on the rocks because it was a stretch of the Chicago lakefront that no one else wanted or cared about. With no lifeguards, people swam without being yelled at, but they also swam without an official watchful eye. We could let our guard down. We could relax. We could be ourselves in completely new ways.

I left the country in 1994. I returned in 2000. I don't remember going to the rocks then, although I probably did. I took them for granted, and then the rocks went away. I didn't appreciate them until they were gone, and Hollywood Beach had become the gay beach. I go to Hollywood Beach on a regular basis. I'm glad we have lifeguard protection until the guy in the boat yells at me to not go in water much deeper than my waist. The sand is soft and lovely. There's a very nice restaurant. People come through periodically, selling popsicles. This is what we wanted. I enjoy it. It's very nice, but there's a part of me that always misses the rocks where we broke the rules just by being ourselves in new ways."

Hanging out at the Belmont Rocks, 1994. Photo by Charles Kass

Relocating to Chicago in 1992, Brian Justice moved into a place on Lake Shore Drive and Irving Park. "I probably started going to the Rocks then and went there for a good five or six years," said Justice.

"When we would say, let's go to the beach, we meant the Rocks. For me, it was a social place and I either went there with people or I met people there. I didn't move around much when I was there. I mostly stayed on the blanket and talked to the people I was there with.

"I thought it was great there was this large public place for gay guys to gather, but at the same time I thought, why are we here? The grass wasn't comfortable, and I never wanted to sit on the Rocks. The place was psychologically and emotionally comfortable, but not physically comfortable. Then it seemed over one summer, everything moved north to Hollywood Beach."

Sun and surf at the Belmont Rocks. Photos courtesy of Paul Kubek.

Victorino first went to the Belmont Rocks in the mid-1990s. "I was at either Roscoe's or Sidetrack, and a guy invited me to go out on his mini yacht. So about five of us went for a ride on his boat. As we neared the Rocks, a couple of guys jumped off the boat and swam to shore. The Rocks was an amazing sight from the water—all the gay men in their Speedos on all those levels—shelves and mounds of them. Seeing that I had a big discovery, that I could be with other gay men and not feel fear. It was a revelation to be with other gay people and not feel threatened."

Victorino shared another favorite Rocks memory, "I went on a date. We went to a Mexican restaurant on Broadway, and they gave us margaritas to go in big Styrofoam cups. It was a hot day. By the time we got to the lake, the sun was setting, and this guy took my hand and led me over to the Rocks. Sitting there, he gave me this glorious head in the middle of the heat wave. I was looking out at the lake and thinking, having my cock sucked al fresco is the best feeling in the world. My wonderful waterfront blowjob.

"When I was in high school, we did a Walkathon that went along the lakefront from North Avenue all the way to Hollywood Beach and then back down to North Avenue again. It's odd to think that we were walking right by this place, one way and then the other, and having no idea that it would be an important place in my life years later."

"I wasn't really a beach goer in my late teens/early 20s, but I used to love to go up to the Rocks with friends and just be around other gay people. It felt exciting to me that there were others. And it was awesome people watching."—Nikki Rinkus.

Ron Volanti, Jr., went to the Belmont Rocks for the first time with friends when he was still in high school. "Then I went to college, and when I came back, I went there a few times with friends. After college, I did an art project with a friend of mine where we met at the Rocks at dawn, and we would bring a breakfast of some sort—Danish or bread and cheese. We had to be early, because dawn was the best time to photograph all the artwork at the lake. The light was incredible. The finished project was published in the *Chicago Tribune* as 'On the Rocks.'

"Most other times I went to the Rocks, I was alone. I like spending time with myself. I would sit there, and people-watch and read, and suntan. But I could be social and meet people if I wanted. There was always the opportunity

Top and bottom photos: Everyone went to the Belmont Rocks on the weekends. Photos courtesy of Mark S.

171

to meet new people there, but if you wanted to be alone, you could sit and other than saying 'Hi,' people wouldn't bother you. They respected that. Nothing was expected of you. The Rocks was my hiding place. It was spending time alone among other people. I felt safe. This was our beach, and the place felt like community."

'On the Rocks, the lakefront is alive with anonymous art,' was featured in the summer section of the *Chicago Tribune Magazine* on Sunday, May 22, 1994. Jeff Lyon's text accompanied the Ann Marie Vlainich photos.

"One day in 1992, Ann Marie Vlainich went to the lakefront with a group of friends to photograph the sunrise.

"As the rocks along the shoreline became gradually bathed in light, Vlainich noticed that they were covered with bold splashes of color and imagery. Unknown artists had left their mark over time, in a style and fashion reminiscent of Stone Age cave paintings or Easter Island statuary.

"A photographer by profession, Vlainich decided that the paintings would make a good project, so she began what would turn into a two-year study of the ghostly artwork. Working her way from Diversey Parkway north to Hollywood Avenue, she captured dozens of images, some painted, some carved.

"I have no idea who created these works, or why they would do it on these lonely rocks,' Vlainich says. 'Obviously, some of them are very talented, and their works very beautiful.'"

"What puzzled Vlainich more was that some of the painters performed year-to-year maintenance on their creations.

"'When I went back the following year, some of the paintings had been painted over in different colors, particularly one of Brigitte Nielsen,' she says.

"The other mystery was the carvings. 'I have no idea how they would even do it," Vlainich says, 'though they sure last. Some stuff goes back to 1958.' ..." (Lyon, 'On the Rocks, the lakefront is alive with anonymous art.' *The Chicago Tribune Magazine*, Sunday, May 22, 1994).

An excerpt from Rick Newberry's memoir, "Trophy"

"During my first summer in Chicago, I discovered the Belmont Rocks. The Belmont Rocks were located on the lakefront between Belmont Harbor and Diversey Harbor, adjacent to Boystown. Huge boulders had been placed there to prevent erosion of the shoreline. During warm months, it was a major gathering place for gay men for cruising, sunbathing, and socializing. I would go there on summer days after work. There would be hundreds of men there of all ages. I met and socialized with several men there. I even hooked up with a few later on. On the lower level of the Rocks, closer to the water, men would often sunbathe nude. On the lawn along the Rocks, there would be large groups of men sunbathing wearing Speedos or thongs. I still laugh about the afternoon a young African American man had a 'boom box' playing music. The Weather Girls 'It's Raining Men' came on. Almost spontaneously, many of the men jumped up and started dancing and singing along!"

Starting around 1993, Richard Dayhoff began what was to be a decade of morning sojourns to the Belmont Rocks before heading to the design studio. "I would usually get there around 6:30 a.m.," said Dayhoff. "I would start my mornings with green tea and meditating and writing with pen and paper at the Rocks. I would be on my same rock every day. My rock was in a little cove right down by the waterline—so tranquil and hidden away. I would touch those rocks and just breathe. I would sit there writing and having my green tea and enjoying a great view of downtown. That was the place that began my day. Most days, I would be there an hour or an hour and a half just writing, drawing, and creating. I sketched a lot of my designs in the margins of those journals. I'm a Scorpio, so I am also very connected to the water. The women's clothing designs I drew there were black, but the design and the fabric tended to be very fluid. I was doing a lot with draping and sort of the quiet luxury that came about because of the Rocks and water influence."

Dayhoff said he loved the freedom of being at the Rocks so early in the day. "If the weather was right, I would be nude. There was a whole community that only came there early in the mornings. We each had our own spots. I went every day of the year, so in the winter or when the Rocks were slippery, I stayed by the top of the Rocks, but I still went there every day."

In the 1980s, the Belmont Rocks were honored by the popular gay dance bar the Broadway Limited (3132 N. Broadway) with a Mr. Belmont Rocks Hot Bod contest.

August 22, 1997, "Gay Chicago"

"Chicago Lesbian Avengers* hosted a candlelight vigil in remembrance of Caitie Mahoney at the Belmont Rocks. Mahoney was a founding member of the Baltimore chapter of Lesbian Avengers. She was killed in a triple murder at a coffee shop in Washington, DC."

*Founded in 1992, the Lesbian Avengers were a direct-action group focused on lesbian visibility and survival. Too impatient for lobbying or letter-writing, these fire-eating secretaries, students, cab drivers, journalists, artists, and teachers joined together to create fabulous street actions that inserted lesbians into public life, forced political change, and redefined dykes as the coolest, most ferocious girls on the block." The group began in New York as a group of six and grew to have more than 60 chapters nationwide. (lesbianavengers.com).

Kevin M. Kleinwachter moved to Chicago from Cincinnati in 1998, settling into a place on Briar. "I had never been to Chicago before, so after I moved into my place, I asked which direction the lake was, and they said, 'Just walk east down Briar until it ends.' So, I walked to where the street ended, went through the park, and under the overpass, and then there was the grass. As I got closer to the lake, I saw a huge rainbow flag painted across two or three of the stones. As I got closer, I thought, 'Oh we have nothing like this in Cincinnati.' I looked around and was sort of like, oh, hey girl. The place was full of gay people."

Kleinwachter offered another reason the Belmont Rocks played an important role in his life. "Up until I went to the Rocks, I was a swimming pool only guy. I had a phobia of slime and algae, and fish. I remember being at the Rocks, and some days the limestone could get so hot in the sun. I heard someone yell, and then I heard a splash and saw that they had jumped in the water. It was so hot that day that I just faced my fear and jumped right into Lake Michigan—and since that day, I have been able to jump into lakes without fear."

❖ ❖ ❖

Rainbow painting on stone. Photo by Stan Z.

❖ ❖ ❖

Photos top and bottom: From the Ferris Bueller events and skipping work to play. Photos courtesy of Wayne Johnson.

"I had always been good about organizing friends to do things," said Wayne Johnson. "So, starting in 1998, again in 1999, and in 2000, I organized and hosted a *Ferris Bueller's Day Off* event. Two out of three of those days involved the Belmont Rocks.

"The concept was simple—just like the movie, basically everyone called in sick to work and went and had fun. I had T-shirts for us each year, and I had special invitations. One year, the invitation came with a tape of suggestions for calling in sick to work."

Johnson continued, "Each of our three Ferris Bueller days involved an outing, a meal, and at the end of the day, we all went to Roscoe's [3354-56 N. Halsted]. At Roscoe's, I would have them play footage or show pictures that I had shot throughout the day. We usually had about 20-30 guys every year who came to the Ferris Bueller outing.

"One year we went for breakfast and then fun and games at the Belmont Rocks, but we played the games they would have at a country fair with a three-legged race and an egg toss, and that kind of thing. Another year it rained, so as an alternative, we went bowling and then for pizza. And the other year we met at the Rocks and then took a bus to Great America.

"A few years later, when I was on the *Today Show*, I did a segment that was directly inspired by those days. We couldn't call it *Ferris Bueller's Day Off* because of the rights, so on the *Today Show* it was called *The Board Meeting*."

"By the summer of 1998, I felt like I had mastered the landscape of gay Chicago," wrote David Jablonowski. A few months prior, I moved into a first-floor apartment on Cornelia with my roommate Aaron. The location was convenient not only for its proximity to the Manhole (in the event that I lost my coat check ticket after an underwear party), but also for shouting lewd remarks at the hot garbage man every Saturday morning. Not kidding. Oh, and also a short walk to the Belmont Rocks.

"I had moved to Chicago only a year earlier, from farm country in upstate New York, spending much of that time explaining the difference between upstate and Manhattan. But now I was beginning my second summer in Chicago. The first had been fraught with delights and terrors—walking out of Roscoe's to see a WANTED poster with images of infamous serial killer Andrew Cunanan. Making my mark up and down Halsted Street—Boystown before the rainbows. Muggy summer days weaving in and out of the Gentry on Halsted (how did those servers survive the humidity in tuxedos?) down the street to newly opened Cocktail, and of course to the original roof deck at Sidetrack. Even random nights at Girlbar (Boybar on Wednesdays!) where the five-dollar pitchers of beer fit my 27-year-old budget perfectly.

"It didn't take long before I knew where to find people like me outside of the bar scene. It was along Lake Michigan, specifically that stretch of shore from Diversey to the Belmont Yacht Club.

"Making an embarrassingly low salary at a second-rate advertising agency, I had no business treating myself to a new Trek mountain bike, but I did the math (on company time) and determined exactly how many bike versus bus rides I would need to take to make my investment pay off. So that's exactly what I did—backpack full of my lunch, gym clothes, and my paper page-a-day calendar—back and forth every Monday through Friday along the bike path.

"As the days started to warm that year, in early May, I saw more and more bikes tipped over just at the edge of the Rocks, so I would follow suit and park mine nearby. I would stand at the top of the Rocks and survey the manscape. Was that old guy with the bad dye job and the great body there again in his threadbare white Speedo? Yes, he was there, his gold bracelets sparkling in the sun, like a gay lighthouse calling boys to the shoreline. There were boys kissing in the daylight. Midwest bodies, thick and hairy, in cutoffs, or sometimes in khakis, coming from work just like me, on each of the layers, each rock closer to the center of the earth. Everyone pretending to work on their tan, or maybe it was just me who was pretending. The water and the washboard abs competed for my attention. Guess which won?

"I met my first boyfriend at the Rocks. It was August that same year, and he was swimming. I was there under the auspices of taking pictures of sailboats with my dad's old 35mm camera. I asked if I could take his picture, and he foolishly agreed. It led to a first date, and then a second, then to a few months of happiness followed by a few more of aggravation—but we remain friends to this day. I took a photo of him on the day we met—to this day, he claims it is the best one taken of him. I'll give credit to that old camera, a bit to the beautiful light, a tiny amount to the photographer, and the rest to the power of the Rocks."

In 1998, *The Chicago Reader* ran the piece 'Forget the Belmont RocksRocks—Hollywood Beach is so out it's in' by Neal Pollack.

The article begins, "By 10 a.m. on Sunday, Hollywood Beach is already filling up with people. The volleyball games start at noon, and the picnics soon after. Everywhere you look—on the grass, in the water, on the sand—there are bodies, male bodies, a sea of beefcake. Single men, couples, groups of five, gangs of twenty or more. Against a backdrop of high-rises, the beach looks like Miami or Honolulu. It's gay Elysium.

"'You have never seen a more densely packed beach in the world,' says one man. 'Not an open inch of sand anywhere. I look at it and think, 'My god! This is incredible! Does anyone go to the Belmont Rocks anymore?'"

"The beach was deserted when Gerry Marcoccia, a 33-year-old government employee, moved to Edgewater in 1990. He would jog or ride his bike along the lake and see maybe 50 people, mostly families, spread across the vast ocean of sparkling-clear sand from Ardmore Avenue to past Bryn Mawr. Marcoccia's friends Bob and Joe would come in from the suburbs on weekends, and he'd take them out to the beach. They'd often mention getting a game of volleyball together. Then one Sunday afternoon in July 1991, Joe and Bob brought a net and strung it between two poles at the south end of the beach. Ten people played that first day. Marcoccia had so much fun that he went out and bought his own net. He called some more friends and had another pickup game the next Sunday.

"'That first year,' he says, 'people would call and say, 'Are you going to be out there?' I finally just said, assume I'm gonna be out there and come join us...'

"Marcoccia didn't know anything about volleyball, and he encouraged reckless abandon in others. They played Jungle Ball without rules and scoring; everyone was invited, regardless of ability or experience..."

"Jungle Ball proved so popular that soon the players became a small but steady club. Mentions of their activities began appearing in the gay gossip magazine *Babble*: "Come to Hollywood Beach and watch the boys play with their balls." In the summer of 1993, during the third season of volleyball, Marcoccia bought a multi-colored gay pride flag and tied it to a tree. ...'I wanted to say this is our place.'" (Neal Pollack, 'Forget the Belmont Rocks, *The Chicago Reader*. July 30, 1998).

In 2018, a full 20 years after publication of the *Reader* piece, Marcoccia reflected on the time. "I moved to Chicago from San Francisco in 1981. When I would go to the Belmont Rocks, I found it unfriendly, boring, and dangerous.

Nobody talked to you unless they were part of their group. There was nothing to do there except lie in the sun or try to go swimming. As someone who used to love to swim, I found the Rocks dangerous to swim at because the rocks were very slippery with algae, and it was hard to get in and out of the water. Also, there were many large hidden boulders in the water to bang your legs or feet on. I cut up my feet and legs on more than one occasion.

"In 1990, I moved up to Edgewater with many of my friends asking me why, because there was nothing to do there compared to in Boystown, which was true. Then, in the summer of 1991, my friends from the suburbs, Bob and Joe, would visit on weekends, and we would go to Hollywood Beach. We would see four empty volleyball courts never being used and the entire beach deserted on some of the most beautiful weekend days of summer. They suggested that we should get some friends together and play some family volleyball (with limited rules and no need for athletic ability). Then one Sunday, they brought their net and we asked friends to join us, and we played all day. I then said that it was so much fun, let's do it every Sunday. Because Bob and Joe lived in the far western suburbs, I didn't want to be dependent on them for their net, so I bought my own. I told everyone that I would be there every Sunday at 2 p.m., weather permitting. (I eventually bought a big rainbow flag to hang from a tree to let everyone know I was there, and it was a safe place for gays.)

"As word got out, more and more people would come, so I kept on buying more equipment each year, which meant again more and more people would come. With the full support of retired Alderman Mary Anne Smith, I was able to get the park district to increase the number of courts from four to six to nine.

"When new people would come, I would go out of my way to welcome them to join us (gay or straight) and tell them we were not there to relive our worst childhood memories of not being athletic enough to enjoy sports. (I was born cross-eyed). I never set out to make Hollywood Beach the gay beach of Chicago, but once I realized what was happening, I ran with it.

"No one was using the beach or courts at the time, and I thought it was about time we had our own actual beach. In addition, as someone who didn't smoke or drink...I didn't want to spend nice weekend days in bars or drinking. At Hollywood Beach, I could play volleyball and enjoy the outdoors, being active and being easily able to go into the water to cool down or go for a swim without it being dangerous.

"At the end of the day of playing volleyball, I would invite whoever was still there to my home for board games and to order out dinner. I sometimes had up to 50 people in my home (luckily, I bought a huge vintage condo on Kenmore).

"I really wanted an alternative to the Belmont Rocks and to have people feel welcome. I wanted to break down barriers. It was also the height of the AIDS epidemic, so it was a way for moments of laughter and joy in the middle of so much pain. Many people who played volleyball are gone now, but many are still with us. I wanted people to look back and have happy memories of their time at Hollywood Beach. I know of several couples who met there and are still together, and people who are still friends who met there over 20 years ago. I wanted it to be a safe and caring place. Unfortunately, over time, it became more and more impersonal as more and more people came to the beach. Also, very athletic and serious volleyball players came, which scared away many of the people I wanted to help feel safe (including myself) who were like me growing up.

"By 1999, Hollywood Beach got so big and impersonal, I was burned out and stopped having anything to do with it. However, I view it as my own little legacy to the gay community. I was there almost every Sunday from 1991 through 1999, all summer long. Eventually, I bought portable sets so that we could play late into the fall and start as early as possible in the spring. One year we started in early March, and in another year we played almost to Thanksgiving. I used to say that I would be out on the beach when you can no longer see your breath in the spring, and will stay out on the beach in the fall until you start seeing your breath. It was some of the best moments of my life as a gay man!"

The Army Corps of Engineers issued a decree—The Rocks were to be demolished as part of the revetment plan to prevent shoreline erosion.

The Belmont Rocks was a unique and integral part of the Chicago LGBTQ scene for over 40 years, but the city was changing, the community was changing, and eventually, most things must come to an end. Activity at the Rocks had dwindled significantly by the early 2000s when the Army Corps of Engineers issued a decree—The Rocks were to be demolished as part of the revetment plan to prevent shoreline erosion.

The Windy City Times reported. "More than 200 people turned out this spring on city plans to destroy the unique place known as 'Belmont Rocks.' For years, it has been a great spot to cool off, to watch and be watched, away from the bike trails and heavily tread lakefront treadways, or a simple spot for solitude. With trees hugging the shore, it brings shade and a sense of escape from the city, right in the middle of everything. All 200 at the Belmont Rocks meeting raised their hands to vote in protest of the replacement design, which invites bikes, but has a huge drop, preventing one from even wetting one's whistle: a soulless concrete runway on the lake.

"Despite the outcry, the city plans on going ahead with the design: letting out bids as early as September, with the area fenced off in the spring for demolition. Officials contend by meeting with locals, they have fulfilled their community obligation—they never promised to actually listen to what the community says. Meanwhile, city plans to destroy Promontory Point, a similar unique lakefront gathering place in Hyde Park, are on hold while an alternative design is in the works for the South Side.

"Let's rock the city. Let's fight for the unique spirit of the Belmont Rocks. Get involved. Don't let them steamroll Belmont Rocks. Petitions will hit the streets soon. Please sign them or Fax the Mayor." (Staff, 'Belmont Rocks,' *Windy City Times*, October 9, 2002).

In another article, "The lakefront revetment plans for the area south of Belmont to Diversey might include a circular garden of limestone rocks removed from the current construction along Lake Michigan.

"That 'circular' could just as easily represent the discussions at a forum on the Belmont Rocks held at Ann Sather's March 6, hosted by new alderman Tom Tunney and with representatives from the city's Department of Environment and Park District.

"As construction equipment sits poised to break ground, many of the 75 or so people at the meeting seemed at the boiling point with city officials who have made promises to involve the community, but who are moving forward regardless of complaints, votes to delay the project, and a petition signed by 1,100 people last summer..." (Staff, 'Rocks Debate Heats Up,' *Windy City Times*, March 12, 2003).

Two weeks later, on March 26, 2003, *The Windy City Times* covered the fate of the Belmont Rocks once again. "Representatives of several community groups met to hammer out a proposal about the planned revetment renovations at the Belmont Rocks in Chicago. They sent a letter to 44th Ward Ald. Tom Tunney last week, and Tunney said he is sending a point-by-point response to the group. But added that the city is set on moving ahead.

"Mayor Daley told Lakeview residents Saturday that he's worked 15 years on this shoreline protection, with money from presidents Clinton and Bush, and he's moving forward. He said he will continue to work on enhancement and accessibility, but said if residents can find money for alternatives, they will look at it—however, he's not willing to delay the project, according to Tunney.

"Neighborhood activist Bob Clarke was the person who sent the letter to Tunney. He hosted the meeting where representatives of Lake View Citizens Council, South East Lake View Neighbors, Save Our Shore, and the Lincoln Park Advisory Council wrote down their goals for the project.

'They seek renovations that are as user-friendly as possible; to increase, not reduce, recreational potential; to provide safe access to and egress from the water; and to enhance, not detract from the feeling of a natural shoreline.

"But with the city starting renovations now, there may be little hope left to fight the bulldozers." (Staff, 'Daley Pushes Ahead on Rocks Despite Protests,' *Windy City Times,* March 26, 2003).

The following week, *The Windy City Times* published 44th Ward Alderman Tom Tunney's responses to the issues raised by the collective of groups.

Excerpts from the letter:

"My primary concerns in relation to revitalization of the revetment between Belmont and Diversey are 1) Preservation of the aesthetic beauty and structural integrity of this valuable lakefront area, 2) Accessibility to the lake and lakefront park areas, and 3) Safety of the public.

"I have communicated...suggestions and concerns from the community to the city and to the Army Corps of Engineers. ...The revised design will incorporate many of the community-suggested 'user-friendly' features, and it will differ from the revetment installed north of Belmont in several important ways, and address our suggestions and concerns in the following ways:

- Preservation of Aesthetic Beauty and Structural Integrity
- The elevation of the revetment section between Belmont and Diversey will be 1 ½ feet lower than the height of the revetment north of Belmont. The city and Army Corps of Engineers have determined that the Belmont to Diversey section does not need to be as high as sections farther north because of less severe wave conditions along the Belmont to Diversey section that do not require a higher 'wave deflection' wall.
- Landscaping will meet the top of the revetment on the park side. This will allow a natural shore-to-lake transition,

maximize the vistas of the lake from the shoreline, and minimize visibility of the revetment structure itself from the shore.

- The revised plan will require strict protection and maximum preservation of existing trees along the project area.
- The Belmont to Diversey revetment will minimize individual step heights to a constant 20 inches, which is lower than the originally proposed 30 inches.
- The Belmont to Diversey structure will incorporate the re-use, to the fullest extent possible, of existing limestone rocks
- The revetment plan will address drainage problems in the parkland behind the rocks that have caused frequent flooding and threatened the topsoil and grass of the park areas.
- I have initiated a discussion with several sectors of the community about the creation of a memorial garden in the park adjacent to the Belmont Rocks. This garden can serve as a place of beauty and reflection, and a place to commemorate the important role that the Belmont Rocks has played in the lives of so many Lakeview residents, their friends, partners, and families. It also may incorporate some of the existing rocks and preserve some of the 'art work' left at the rocks over many years.
- In order to make the area around the former gun club at the south end of the Belmont to Diversey beachfront safe and usable for the public, the city plan will provide additional landfill in this area. This new landfill will be a significant benefit to our Lakeview area beachfront. It will create between 1 ½ to 2 ½ acres of new lakefront lands made up of a combination of new open green space and the revitalized revetment.

Safety

- I strongly believe that this section of the lakefront, and the parklands adjacent to it, must be safe for all who use them.

- The revised city plan will add safety ladders at regular intervals to allow easier egress between shore and water. These will be painted yellow to ensure increased safety and enhanced visibility.
- The revetment will rectify major safety hazards that exist along the current sea wall by:
  - replacing sections of the current rocks that are unstable and may be resting in positions that make them precarious and unsafe for people to walk along them.
  - restoring stability where large sections of the rocks, or the foundations beneath them, have collapsed, or where wave action over the years has created dangerous caverns under the rocks.
  - eliminating hazards caused by the numerous and large gaps and holes that currently exist in long sections of the rocks. These hazards make walking along them dangerous for many, and impossible for some.
  - reinforcing the stability and enhancing the usefulness of the parkland behind the sea wall.

Currently, large areas of parkland behind the rocks are threatened or left unprotected because of gaps that have developed between rocks because of cave-ins. Years of flooding over the rocks has washed out topsoil and created sink holes under some of the parkland behind the rocks.

- Eliminating fallen rocks and semi-submerged debris in the water adjacent to the rocks. This will reduce hazards for people (and their pets) who swim, kayak, windsurf, or enjoy other recreation in these areas.

Accessibility

- I believe that the rocks, the park areas adjacent to them, and the lake itself should be as fully accessible as possible to all who want to use and enjoy them.
- The revetment from Belmont to Diversey, and the paths to it, will provide universal access with an even grade of the revetment to the shoreline.

- The revised plan will nearly triple the portion of the Belmont to Diversey shoreline that consists of people-friendly, raised-stone 'toe berms.' These will add a more seamless and synergistic visual and physical transition from the shore to the revetment, and to the lake, and increase direct lake access for the public.

- The revised plan will relocate paths going to the rocks in a manner that preserves maximum park recreational space and uses alternate, natural materials as much as possible.

- The construction projects will be phased to minimize the work area and to maximize the amount of park space available for public use during the project.

- Additional ramps will also be installed that are consistent with ADA requirements.

(Staff, 'Tunney Issues Statement on Belmont Rocks work.' *Windy City Times*, April 2, 2003).

❖ ❖ ❖

Rock with graffiti saved from demolition. Author's collection.

As the late Charlotte Newfeld (1930-1922) recalled in 2017, "When we lost the battle to keep the step stone rock revetment, it was important to save the stones with messages and great paintings. Tom Tunney and I were there on a very early morning when the removal of the limestone Rocks was to start. We picked out Rocks to be saved and replanted on the new revetment. The 'Hard Hat' in charge did not want to save any words he thought obscene. I insisted that all rocks with human markings be saved, and Tom went leaping around and marking for saving. Unfortunately, many fell apart in attempts to save them. What remains are along the lake south of Belmont."

Bruce Dunlap beside a piece of the original Belmont Rocks artwork. This was one of the few surviving artworks at the Rocks. Photo courtesy of B. Dunlap.

"Charlotte was very upset about putting in the concrete revetment," said former Alderman Tunney. "Charlotte was adamant that if there was a concrete revetment that we would put the top layer of the concrete with the old rocks. Those rocks were put in storage and brought back out. The other surviving rocks were the conversation circles that still exist today."

Tom Tunney moved to the North Side of Chicago in the spring of 1980. "I had started in February at Ann Sather and worked there with the intent to buy it. I was always hyper-focused on the restaurant being successful. I had a loan to buy the place, and the interest rates were high, so I was working breakfast, lunch, and dinner seven days a week. I didn't have much time for anything else. The restaurant also provided my social outlet. I wasn't really a bar person, especially since I had to be up and at the restaurant for breakfast.

"In 1984/1985, we moved the restaurant a few doors down on Belmont from the old building to a new, larger building with an upstairs area. We had the second floor for banquets and catering, and over the years, we hosted many funerals and memorials in that space. Many of those were for people who died of AIDS.

"I was a freshman alderman when the Rocks were being redone with the concrete revetments. There was an outpouring of people who were against it and cited the history there, but the Army Corps of Engineers didn't care. It was what needed to be done.

"That was really when I first thought of an AIDS Garden," continued Tunney. "Other cities had them. When I proposed the idea, Mayor Daley was fine with it and the Park District was fine with it, but the money wasn't there, so we were going to have to raise the funds privately. In 2005/2006, we had a landscaping plan done. Then, in 2007/2008, a recession hit, and the project was put on the shelf for a bit. Then I became involved with the sculpture program for the city and expanded that from Lincoln Park to Lincoln Park/Lakeview.

"By then, it was 2015 or so. Rahm [Mayor Emanuel] and the Park District were still fine with the idea of an AIDS Garden, but again, it was a matter of the funding. That's when the idea came for the Keith Haring piece, *Self-Portrait*—it came from working with the sculpture program for the city. Fred Eichner and I paid $500,000 for the Haring sculpture. The city paid for the base for it. With an image to associate with the garden, it became easier to get the idea out there. The Haring sculpture became the garden's marquee and a catalyst for moving forward. Then [Illinois State Rep.] Greg Harris came through with a grant from the state. After that, the AIDS Garden became a mission for Greg and I. There was a sense of, if we don't do this, it's not going to happen. Our generation needs to get this done."

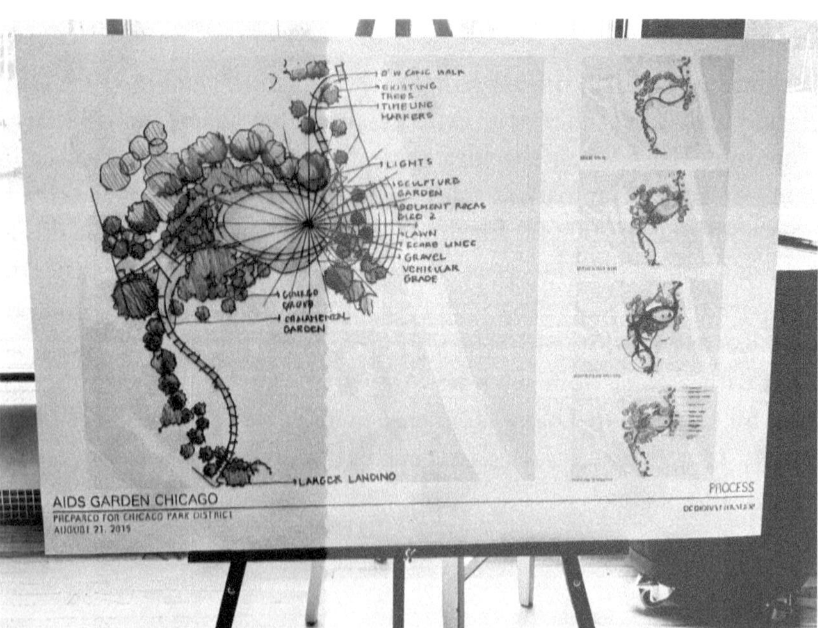

Top and bottom photos: Initial plans made for the AIDS Garden Chicago.

On November 14, 2019, the AIDS Garden Chicago group issued a statement. "The Chicago Parks Foundation today announced that the first phase of the new AIDS Garden Chicago will be complete this Fall with the unveiling of a specially commissioned 30-foot-high sculpture, *Self-Portrait,* by iconic HIV/AIDS activist and artist, the late Keith Haring. ...AIDS Garden Chicago will be the city's first public monument to memorialize the early days of Chicago's HIV epidemic and to honor those who continue to fight against the disease today. ...The new 2.5-acre public lakefront garden will be located along Lake Michigan just south of Belmont Harbor, at the original location of the 'Belmont Rocks,' a space where the local gay community gathered between the 1960s and 1990s.

"The fight against HIV/AIDS represents more than a health epidemic: it symbolizes a time in our history when the LGBTQ+ and ally communities came together in the face of tragedy," said Mayor Lori E. Lightfoot. "We lost countless neighbors and friends, and relatives over the years, but we have made significant strides in combating the virus. What was one of the darkest moments of the 20th century has given way to a blooming garden of hope and love; this new AIDS Garden Chicago will serve as a permanent reminder of how far we have come and as a way to honor those who continue the work of getting to zero new HIV infections."

"The Chicago Parks Foundation is so honored to be a part of this historic and legacy project for the city and all the communities and individuals who have been affected and still are living with HIV/AIDS. We are far from eradicating the disease, but this garden and iconic Keith Haring sculpture will serve as a beacon of hope and unity for all. This is truly a park with a purpose and a message," said Chicago Parks Foundation Executive Director Willa Lang.

"We have worked closely with some of our longtime community leaders, held meetings with various community groups, and are now excited to start phase one of this overdue project," said Alderman Tom Tunney. "*Self-Portrait's* new home at AIDS Garden Chicago, in the 44th Ward, is a small but powerful way to continue talking about the epidemic as we fight to bring both HIV infections and AIDS-related deaths to zero.

"Bold, bright green and nearly three stories high, *Self-Portrait* will be the largest iteration of this popular sculpture that has ever been fabricated, and the Chicago Parks Foundation expects it to be the Garden's signature anchor and gathering point. Working with the Chicago Park District and designed by landscape architects Design Workshop, AIDS Garden Chicago is set to be completed in 2020 and will include unique areas designed for reflection, education, honor, and pride. Visitors will be guided with markers and milestones through a variety of intimate and collective garden spaces to be coordinated and maintained by community gardeners still in formation. This park garden will provide a sensory nature experience; the most notable being a memorable grove of Gingko trees and a perennial garden of natural plantings at the entrance. A serpentine path will be the site for future temporary art installations organized by community partners.

"*Self-Portrait* is provided to AIDS Garden Chicago through a generous gift from the Keith Haring Foundation, with personal financial support from Alderman Tom Tunney that was matched by the Alphawood Foundation Chicago. Rosenthal Fine Art, which facilitated the conversation with the Haring Foundation, was established here in 1986 and has most recently been dedicated to making art more accessible to the public through partnerships with private developers and city agencies.

"Alderman Tom Tunney and the Chicago Parks Foundation thank all the valuable partners still in formation and continuing to grow, including the Keith Haring Foundation, AIDS Foundation of Chicago, Alphawood Foundation Chicago, Center on Halsted, Friends of the Parks, Howard Brown Health, and the Legacy Project. The Chicago Parks Foundation welcomes additional financial partners to help bring the project to completion."

A steady course was charted for completion, and things seemed on schedule—then came the COVID epidemic. COVID put everything on hold, but only for a year. On June 2, 2021, various city and state officials each grabbed a shovel and a hard hat, in assorted rainbow colors, for the official groundbreaking to commence work on what was to become AIDS Garden Chicago.

At the groundbreaking ceremony, 44th Ward Alderman Tom Tunney referred to the Belmont Rocks as sacred ground, describing the space as "the place where many of the LGBT community socialized and organized. It is also the place, unfortunately, [where] many scattered the ashes of loved ones."

Landscaping, planting, and various garden installations promptly followed the groundbreaking.

Groundbreaking at AIDS Garden Chicago. Author's collection.

June 2, 2022, was the ribbon-cutting to officially open AIDS Garden Chicago. It was exactly one year since the groundbreaking.

At the opening ceremony, which coincided with the start of Pride Month, Mayor Lightfoot stepped to the microphone. "I'm honored to officially cut the ribbon on AIDS Garden Chicago in a place that means so much for our LGBTQ+ community. As we memorialize those we've lost to the HIV epidemic and inspire those who continue to fight the disease, it has never been more important to immortalize Belmont Rocks' legacy as a safe space where people could gather, support one another, and be their full selves. I hope that residents and visitors alike will continue gathering here at our city's newest symbol of liberation, individuality, and hope."

In his PositiveAware.com recap of the AIDS Garden Chicago opening, Jeff Berry shared another portion of Mayor Lightfoot's speech. "I came to Chicago in the mid-eighties, trying to find my own place in the world but not yet living openly. After coming out in law school, I found my identity in this

Photos top and bottom: The ribbon cutting and official opening of AIDS Garden Chicago. Author's collection.

city, and this spot really means a lot to me personally. I came here after my first Pride parade, and I was amazed to see what felt like a sea of beautiful, diverse humanity, hanging out, dancing, playing music, barbecuing. I'd never seen or experienced anything like that before. It gave me a sense of assurance that I was making the right decision by coming out and embracing who I was, something I'd known since I was a child, but finally having the courage to say this is who I am, this is the life I'm going to lead, and I'm never going to look back. I'm always going to look forward. It was an incredible time."

At the ceremony, State Representative Greg Harris, who was diagnosed with HIV in 1988 and AIDS in 1990, also addressed the crowd. "I'd love to be here today consecrating this ground, looking out at a sea of my friends, associates, colleagues, and the people who used to hang out here with me, but most of them are dead. This is a memorial to those guys and the thousands of folks who died from AIDS."

Jonathan "Yoni" Pizer became involved with AIDS Garden Chicago after being approached by 44th Ward Alderman Tom Tunney. "Alderman Tunney was looking for someone to usher the Garden from the groundbreaking phase, through the ribbon-cutting phase, and beyond—so I became the Board Chair for the AIDS Garden. The Garden is such a special place—a reminder of how this community responded when we were met with a challenge and how we joined together. It is a place to honor those lost to the disease as well as those who continue to be impacted by AIDS and HIV. AIDS Garden Chicago is a park with a purpose."

The Keith Haring sculpture 'Self Portrait' at AIDS Garden Chicago. Author's collection.

Rocks of Ages

Chicago summers are short. Short as the short shorts, cut-offs, and Speedos worn by the men who congregated on the Belmont Rocks. Kissing and hugging, drinking and drugging, dancing and

romancing. Big baskets and picnic baskets. Hair gel, sweat, deodorant, cologne, scents mingling with fried chicken and hot dogs, cigarettes and pot smoke. Every sense activated and vibrating.

The music, BPM, divas' voices, reverberated off steel, concrete, brick, and glass high rises, rose high as the highest balconies. Depending on what floor you lived on, you might not need binoculars

to observe the homoerotic display. Colorful beach towels, blankets, even tablecloths spread out for maximum exposure to sunlight and the light that burned in men's eyes in the Chicago summer heat

when skin was bared and tanned. Skin smooth and
coated in suntan lotion, skin tattooed in symbols,
images, words. Lake waves create a shimmer effect,
reflect the sun; a flat, wet, and shifting mirror ball.

Language fails to effectively gauge the incalculable
loss, numbers staggering. A limestone garden
planted where they used to gather and brightly
glimmer, a permanent memorial to queer lives lived.

—Gregg Shapiro

Soaking up the sun at the Belmont Rocks. Photo from Gay Chicago *courtesy of the Legacy Project.*

Acknowledgements

Thanks to the folks of *Windy City Times*, *Gay Chicago*, *Gay Life*, *Chicago Outlines* and all the additional members of the Chicago LGBT press. Thank you for your service and for chronicling our history. My work would be impossible without your efforts.

Thanks to Chicago's two excellent LGBTQ community resources, the Gerber Hart Library and Archives and the Leather Archives and Museum for being repositories of our stories and our history.

Thanks to Ian and Sukie at Rattling Good Yarns Press for their continued guidance and support of my work. You are the heart and soul of independent publishing.

My deepest gratitude to the dozens of folks who shared their memories of life at the Belmont Rocks, your contribution was deeply appreciated. Telling the story of the Belmont Rocks was truly a community effort.

Thank you to the founders, maintainers, and supporters of Chicago AIDS Garden for recognizing and honoring the importance of the Belmont Rocks area.

And finally, love to my husband Carl for his endless support.

About the Author

The author at the Belmont Rocks. Photo: author's collection.

Queer historian and writer Owen Keehnen is the author of several fiction and nonfiction titles. His books of LGBT Chicago history include *Dugan's Bistro and the Legend of the Bearded Lady, Man's Country More Than a Bathhouse*, and *Gay Chicago Memories 1300 N. Wells*. He coauthored, with Tracy Baim, the biographies of three Chicago LGBTQ community legends — *Leatherman: The Legend of Chuck Renslow, Jim Flint: The Boy From Peoria*, and *Vernita Gray: From Woodstock to the White House*. He worked with St Sukie de la Croix on the *Tell Me About It* series, a gay studies trilogy chronicling the milestones in LGBTQ lives. Keehnen is the cofounder of the LGBTQ history/education organization, the Legacy Project and was on the founding committee for AIDS Garden Chicago. He was inducted into the Chicago LGBT Hall of Fame in 2011. He lives in Chicago with his husband, Carl, and their dogs, Vince and Daisy.